CASSELL'S GUIDE TO
punctuation

CASSELL'S GUIDE TO

punctuation

loreto todd

CASSELL&CO

First published in the UK in 1995 by
Cassell & Co.
Wellington House
125 Strand
London WC2R 0BB
First paperback edition 1997
This edition 2001

British Library Cataloguing-in-Publication Data
A catalogue record for this book is available from the British Library

ISBN 0-304-35786-3

Typeset by MS Filmsetting Limited, Frome, Somerset
Printed and bound in Great Britain by Bookmarque

Contents

Acknowledgements

Many friends, students and colleagues have helped in the writing of this book. Some have asked questions; some have revealed uncertainties: and some have commented on earlier drafts. I am grateful to all of them for their advice and support.

I should like to express particular thanks to Mary Penrith, especially for help with proof-reading; to Tony Richards, University Radiation Protection Service, for commenting on the punctuation needs of scientists; to George Cave and Carol Clarke for their wealth of comments as educators; to Wayne Paton, for tracking down a translation of Anton Chekhov's 'The Exclamation Mark'; and finally, to Rosie Anderson, Hannah Sambrook and Nigel Wilcockson for their editorial advice and helpful suggestions on layout.

Symbols

Symbols are used sparingly in this *Guide*. The commonest are:
- $\rightarrow$ means 'can be rewritten as'. Thus $A \rightarrow B + C$ means that A can be rewritten as $B + C$.
- $<$ means 'derives/derived from'.
- $>$ means 'becomes/became'.
- $*$ precedes a usage that is unacceptable today.
- $?$ precedes a doubtful usage.

Section 1

Background

The need for punctuation

The word punctuation was, according to the *Oxford English Dictionary*, first recorded in 1539. It comes from Latin *punctatio* (making a point, marking with points) and *punctum* (a point), both words deriving ultimately from the Latin verb *pungere* meaning 'to pierce, prick or puncture'.

Punctuation involves the use of spacing, size of letters and a set of standardized marks to separate structural units in written texts and thus to clarify meaning by guiding our reading. Well used, it is like clear enunciation in speech and may be thought of as the equivalent of perfect articulation. Until the eighteenth century, punctuation was based on speech pauses and so was an aid to reading aloud. Over the last two centuries, however, its use has been governed by grammatical structure, making it particularly appropriate to silent reading. Heavy punctuation, including the widespread use of commas, colons and semicolons, was common in the past. Today, lighter punctuation is more usual. This is in part due to the modern tendency to use shorter sentences.

Before 1960, virtually all children in Britain learned to punctuate at school. Most of them, it is true, were uncertain about colons, but many were confident in their use of commas, full stops, question marks and inverted commas. During the 1970s and 1980s, punctuation was rarely taught in schools, and, not surprisingly, even the brightest A-level English students had difficulties with it. According to school inspectors, they frequently used 'the comma as a catch-all to replace the colon, semi-colon and full stop' (*Sunday Times*, 26 December 1993). Punctuation, like traditional grammar, was seen by some educationists as an unnecessary brake on children's spontaneity and creativity. There is little evidence that children today write more spontaneously or creatively than their parents. There is considerable evidence, however, that they write less accurately. Expecting children to write well while depriving them of the rules of language is the equivalent of expecting people to drive well without giving them access to the Highway Code. In neither case should lack of control be confused with freedom.

Punctuation is a necessary feature of the written medium. It is analogous to intonation, pitch, rhythm, speed and pausing in speech. It helps us to write with clarity and to read with understanding. Just as there are individual ways of talking, there are personal and even idiosyncratic methods of punctuation, but we must understand and share the basic rules if we are to communicate unambiguously. It is like spelling in that it may *seem* unsystematic. Like spelling, however, it is rule-governed and the more we know about it, the better we can appreciate it.

Let us look a little more closely at the written medium and at the need for punctuation. When we write English, we write each line from left to right:

```
------ > ------ > ------ > ------ > ------ >
------ > ------ > ------ > ------ > ------ >
------ > ------ > ------ > ------ > ------ >
```

There is nothing particularly logical or natural about this system. We might equally well have chosen to write alternate lines from different directions, beginning with left to right:

```
------ > ------ > ------ > ------ > ------ >
------ < ------ < ------ < ------ < ------ <
------ > ------ > ------ > ------ > ------ >
```

or we might write from right to left, like writers of Arabic or Hebrew:

```
------ < ------ < ------ < ------ < ------ <
------ < ------ < ------ < ------ < ------ <
------ < ------ < ------ < ------ < ------ <
```

or we might have alternated but started the first line from right to left:

Of course, we might also have chosen to write from the top to the bottom of the page, as the Chinese do, or from the bottom to the top or even in a circle. What is important is shared knowledge of the chosen convention. With the exception of a few well-known palindromes, such as:

Able was I ere I saw Elba

a knowledge of the order (from left to right) is essential to our understanding of the written language. Equally essential is the need for spaces, if we are to distinguish between:

independent countries

and:

in dependent countries.

And a capital letter, space and an apostrophe allow us to distinguish between:

impolite

and:

I'm polite.

How did punctuation start?

If we exclude cave drawings and scratches on bones, our earliest written records are less than six thousand years old. They were made by the Sumerians to keep track of their commercial dealings. This writing system was pictographic, that is, it used pictures to represent words or ideas. We use pictograms today for international road signs and for public conveniences. A modern hotel may simplify its description by using such pictograms as:

which mean that the hotel has 135 bedrooms and a lift, as well as television sets, radios, telephones and coffee-making facilities in each bedroom.

Such a system can have advantages over word-based writing: one stylized picture of a woman can indicate that washing and toilet facilities are available for women, whether they call themselves *Damen, femmes, Frauen, senores, signoras, mná* or *women.*

From time to time we need to learn new symbols. A good example of this is the use of '0' and '1' on electrical switches throughout the European Community. This technique, based on the binary system, uses '0' for 'off' and '1' for 'on'.

Gradually, pictograms were replaced by word-based systems, which did not have either spaces or punctuation marks. Early writing was concerned with commerce, however, rather than with abstractions, and so the system worked adequately. As soon as it began to be used for non-practical matters, modifications to the system were made.

From the fifth century BC onwards there are Greek examples of words being separated from each other by series of vertically arranged dots, usually two (:) or three (⋮). Greek dramatists such as Euripides (?480-406BC) and Aristophanes (?448-380BC) introduced graphological symbols to help with the production and interpretation of their plays. Such symbols allowed the writers to indicate different speakers, to suggest suitable breath pauses for the chorus and to divide speeches into three lengths, known as *commas, colons* and *periods.* A short piece or comma was marked by a mid point (·) after the last letter of the section; a longer piece or colon was marked by a low point (.); and the longest passage or period was marked by a high point (˙) after the last letter. The modern metaphorical use of *high point* to mean a time of great happiness or achievement in one's life is related to punctuation. Aristotle (384-322BC) was familiar with such signs and also made use of the *paragraphos*, a horizontal line drawn under the first words of a new topic.

Latin texts also used punctuation marks, but these show considerable variation. For almost three hundred years, until AD200, dots, usually in twos (:) and threes (⋮), were sometimes used between words. New topics or paragraphs were indicated by placing one or two words in the left-hand margin, that is, by a system that is the opposite of indentation. The fourth-century grammarian, Aelius Donatus, whose writings inspired the teaching of grammar for over a thousand years, often used the Greek system of high, mid and low points for marking passages of different lengths. Donatus did not separate words from each other, but some of his contemporaries indicated the end of a sentence by the use of a space or a point or by using a large letter at the start of the new sentence.

St Jerome (Eusebius Hieronymus, AD?347–?420) was one of Donatus's students. He was a scholar and a monk and spent most of his life producing the Vulgate, the Latin version of the Bible. Because Jerome believed that he was dealing with the inspired word of God, he and his co-workers evolved a punctuation system that permitted effective, unambiguous reading and chanting of the Latin text. The biblical text was divided into phrases:

1 In the beginning God created the heaven and the earth.

2 And the earth was without form, and void; and darkness was upon the face of the deep. And the Spirit of God moved upon the face of the waters.

3 And God said, 'Let there be light'; and there was light.

Our example of the first three verses of the Book of Genesis is in English with modern punctuation, but it helps to illustrate how St Jerome divided the Bible into breath-length units. He did not use numbers but each phrase began with a letter which projected into the margin.

Until the early seventh century, most scribes used the same sized letters for the entire text. Usually, these were *uncials*, large rounded letters, called uncials because they were originally an uncial, or one Roman inch high. These letters are also called *majuscules* or capital letters. (The word comes from Latin and is related to 'major'.) Shorter letters were known as *half-uncials*. From this time on, there was a tendency to use two sizes of letters, with *minuscules* or small letters preferred. At about the same time as the introduction of lower-case letters, monks began to use three other techniques that are familiar to us: they used small spaces between words, larger spaces between sentences, and capital letters for the first word in a sentence. These innovations are to be seen in *The Book of Kells*, a Latin manuscript of the four gospels, written between the eighth and the tenth centuries.

It was another monk, this time a man from York, called Alcuin (Ealhwine, ?735–804), who extended the inventory of punctuation marks, making it almost modern in appearance. Alcuin was an adviser to the Holy Roman Emperor, Charlemagne (?742–814). Charlemagne's empire extended from the Ebro (Spain) to the Elbe (Germany), and his court at Aachen became a centre for commerce, learning and spirituality. Alcuin, like Jerome, was interested in the accurate writing and reading of the Bible. He helped standardize spelling and introduced a system of minuscules. In addition, he used a variety of marks to help monks with their Gregorian chant. One point was used to mark the end of a phrase; a group of points indicated the end of a sentence; a raised point (*punctus elevatus*) showed when a higher note or a rise in pitch was required; and a *punctus interrogativus* indicated a gradual lowering of pitch before rising again.

It is hard to overestimate the value of the innovations in punctuation brought about by Jerome and Alcuin. They were mainly interested in ensuring the accuracy of the word of God, but they provided a mechanism that became increasingly valuable to merchants and scholars as well as to clerics, because it marked syntactic units as well as being an aid to accurate reading.

Alcuin's system was used throughout Charlemagne's empire and was employed by scribes for over three hundred years. Modifications continued to be introduced, however, in the search for clarity. A hyphen (-) began to be used in the tenth century when a word had to be broken at the end of a line. Occasionally, a double hyphen or equal sign (=) served the same purpose; a colon (:) became a regular marker of the end of a biblical verse; a circumflex (>) could indicate the end of a subordinate clause, showing that the pitch of the voice should rise in preparation for the main clause; the letter 'c' from *capitulum*, 'little head', indicated the start of a paragraph or sentence; and a virgule (/) marked a short stop.

All of these punctuation devices were in place by about 1400, but they were not always systematically adhered to, even in monastic scriptoria. The writing of non-liturgical texts shows much less regularity in the use of punctuation marks. In an attempt to prevent potential ambiguities or fraudulently inserted marks, writers of legal documents tended to avoid punctuation altogether, a tendency that continues to influence contemporary legalese, such as the language of house deeds:

> This Conveyance is made the twenty first day of December One thousand nine hundred and thirty four between Pickard and Company Limited whose registered office is situate at Dorrington Street in the City of Leeds Builders and Contractors (hereinafter called the Vendors) of the one part and Harry W***** of 39 Lofthouse Place in the said City of Leeds Foreman and Doris Mary W***** his wife (hereinafter called the Purchasers) of the other part whereas the vendors are seised in fee simple in possession free from incumbrance of and in the property herinafter described and intended to be hereby conveyed and have agreed to sell the same to the purchasers for a like estate in fee simple in possession free from incumbrances for the sum of . . .

Geoffrey Chaucer (?1340–1400), the poet, suggests the often haphazard system of punctuation used in reproductions when he worries that his verse might be misunderstood because of being poorly transcribed:

> And for ther is so gret diversite
> In English and in writyng of oure tonge,
> So preye I God that non miswryte the,
> Ne mysmetre for defaute of tonge.
>
> (*Troilus and Criseyde*, 1793–96)

Chaucer's worries are more easily understood when we study the early printed works of William Caxton (?1422–91), who set up the first printing press in England in 1477. Caxton made a considerable contribution to the standardizing of grammar and spelling, but his use of punctuation is unsystematic.

The development of printing in the fifteenth century made written texts more widely available than they had ever been in the past, and it also brought about the need for a standard system of punctuation. This need was met during the fifteenth and sixteenth centuries by the Venetian printer, Aldus Manutius (1450–1515), and his grandson. These printers aimed to produce fine editions of the classics and, in the process, they developed a plan of punctuation that is the basis of our modern system. They realized that books would be read silently in future, so they abandoned marks such as the *punctus elevatus*, which had been introduced for liturgical readers and cantors. They systematically used the virgule (/) and the colon (:) for marking off short phrases; they lowered the virgule and curved it so that it began to look like a modern comma; they employed the semicolon and full stop at the end of sentences and paragraphs; they made occasional use of round brackets ( ) to enclose additional information; and when, by 1660, the dash, exclamation mark and quotation marks had been added, our modern system was virtually in place.

The one punctuation mark we have not so far referred to is the *apostrophe*, probably the most misused device in the language. Its use began to be standardized in the sixteenth century, when it was employed to indicate the omission of letters:

> Thou lie out on't, sir, and therefore 'tis not yours. For my
> part, I do not lie in't, and yet it is mine.   (*Hamlet*)

and to mark the plurals of nouns, especially of borrowed words ending in a vowel:

> We doe confess Errata's   (Leonard Lichfield, 1641)

> Comma's are used   (Philip Luckcombe, 1771)

The use of the apostrophe to mark possession was intermittent until the end of the eighteenth century. The possessive apostrophe appears rarely in the early quartos of Shakespeare, and only occasionally in John Milton. It proved useful, however, as a method of distinguishing between:

> the boy's plan

and:

> the boys' plan

and it permits the unambiguous reading of the first part of such a sentence as:

> *The boys plan to excavate the ruin is ill-advised.

By the nineteenth century, therefore, grammarians were agreed that the apostrophe should be used for two purposes: to indicate the omission of letters and to mark possession.

To say that grammarians had fixed rules for the apostrophe is not, however, to claim that it was always used correctly. Many Victorians, like their modern counterparts, used the apostrophe to indicate plurality, as in *motto's (instead of mottoes), while others saw no reason to include the possessive apostrophe in children's clothes, where there was no possibility of confusion or ambiguity. Just as there has never been a vintage year for the English language, there has never been a time when all writers knew what was required and followed the conventions.

The above is a brief and, necessarily, superficial treatment of a complex system of marking. We should, however, make one further generalization. Punctuation is taken for granted now. It has become as familiar to readers as the alphabet. Ideally, this familiarity should breed respect not contempt. Well used, punctuation marks are like the rhythms and resonances of a human voice: they aid comprehension, help us to avoid ambiguity, and allow us to express ourselves with subtlety and precision.

The names and uses of punctuation marks

The punctuation marks currently employed in English are dealt with in detail in Section 2. The majority of the most widely used ones, and their names, date back to the fifteenth century or before and many are found, in recognizable uses, in the writings of the English author George Puttenham (?1520–?1601) and his contemporaries. Most of the terms were adapted from Greek, sometimes through Latin and French, and used with modified meanings. The comma is our most frequently used punctuation mark and, although disparaged by Samuel Johnson's Dictionary as 'the least of the marks of punctuation', its history is reasonably representative of punctuation marks generally. The word comes from Greek *kómma* and meant 'a piece cut off' and, later, 'a phrase or short clause'. It was adopted into Latin as *comma* and borrowed into English in the sixteenth century. In its progress from Greek to English, the word began to refer to the symbol used rather than to the piece of text it had once marked off or cut out.

Modern personal computers have widened the range of orthographic devices open to us. In writing in the past, emphasis could be indicated by position, by punctuation marks, by underlining or by the use of capital letters. Today, it can be indicated by all of these plus emboldening, italicization or even by the use of an unusual font or innovative layout.

Using punctuation marks: an overview

Punctuation is currently used to help clarify meaning in the written medium. It does this by marking words or groups of words into units that can be linked by commas, for example:

Shakespeare wrote *Hamlet*, *King Lear*, *Macbeth* and *Othello*.

or separated by full stops:

Shakespeare wrote over thirty plays. He was a contemporary of Christopher Marlowe.

The importance of spacing, capitalization, the use of the apostrophe, the question mark and obliques can be illustrated by such examples as:

whosthepoembybyron

which could mean all or any of the following:

'Who's the poem by?' 'Byron.'
'Who's the poem by? Byron?'
'Who's the poem by?' 'By Ron.'
'Who's the poem by? By Ron?'

Similar ambiguities are apparent in:

whathaveyouheardaboutdistemper

which could be:

What have you heard about distemper?

or:

What have you heard about Di's temper?

If punctuation did not exist, only context would allow us to distinguish between *fool's cap* and *foolscap*, or even between *manslaughter* and *man's laughter*. In spite of the obvious advantages of using punctuation, many legal documents, as we mentioned above, avoid almost all marks except full stops and capital letters. A typical publisher's contract of the 1990s, for example, includes the following clause:

> 12.1 The decisions on the paper printing binding text design jacket and/or cover design manner and extent of advertising and the number and distribution of free copies of the Work and the price quantity and terms of sale of the first and every later edition of the Work and the exploitation of the rights granted in clauses 3 and 15 shall be left to the judgement and sole discretion of the Publishers.

Initially, it is not easy to decide whether the clause intends 'paper-printing' or 'paper, printing'. Equally ambiguous is the grouping 'text design jacket', which could be interpreted as 'text, design, jacket' or 'text-design, jacket' or even 'text, design-jacket'. The reason for avoiding commas in contracts derives, ironically, from an appreciation of their significance. The insertion of a comma or an apostrophe into sentences such as:

She was sick and tired of all the visitors.
I'll go because I'm good and ready to go.
He walked on his head in the air.
You'd probably find the cats there with her.

radically affects the meaning:

>She was sick, and tired of all the visitors.
>I'll go because I'm good, and ready to go.
>He walked on, his head in the air.
>You'd probably find the cat's there with her.

When we think of punctuation marks, we usually think of them as individual items such as commas, which can help us to write with clarity. Further thought will suggest, however, that punctuation is like a current in water: of vital significance but often overlooked.

Some punctuation marks appear singly; others can occur either singly or in pairs; while others can occur only in pairs. The punctuation marks that appear singly are the full stop, the exclamation mark, the question mark, ellipsis, the semicolon, the colon, the apostrophe, the asterisk and the hyphen. Commas and dashes may appear either singly or in pairs. Brackets and quotation marks appear only in pairs.

Simplifying somewhat, we can say that there are two main types of punctuation marks: those that mark the end of an utterance, and those that separate one part of a sentence from another. We have called these *terminators* and *separators*. (For an explanation of these terms see pp. 120–22.) Punctuation marks that can function as terminators are ellipses, exclamation marks, full stops and question marks:

>Reader, I married him …
>That's terrible!
>John did it.
>Who did it?

All terminators incorporate a full stop and they follow the last word without an intervening space:

>We did it!
>*We did it !

The separators can, in fact, be divided into three subsets: separators 1, separators 2 and separators 3. Separators 1 can be used either singly, to separate one part of a sentence from the rest, or in pairs, to enclose part of a sentence. The punctuation marks that can function as separators 1 are commas, dashes and obliques. As we have seen, the comma is the most frequently used:

He was kind, gentle and industrious.
The women, who wore seat belts, were safe.

Several single commas can, of course, occur in the one sentence:

> But there he was, always, a steaming hulk of an uncle, his braces straining like hawsers, crammed behind the counter of the tiny shop at the front of the house, and breathing like a brass band; or guzzling and blustery in the kitchen over his gutsy supper, too big for everything except the great black boats of his boots.   (Dylan Thomas, 'A Story', 1955)

Dashes and obliques tend to have more limited roles:

> A selection of properties currently available – full details are available on all the properties.
> It is not his business – or the governor's business – to do so.

> A student wishing to apply should submit his/her résumé by 28 April.
> The symbol /b/ represents the initial sound in 'back'.

Separators 2 appear singly. They are apostrophes, colons, ellipses, hyphens and semicolons:

> If he stuck up for me after I'd been framed ...

> The state of the language in any age provides the basis from which a writer can work: he cannot direct the language, he can only employ it, and the range of possible employment, though wide enough, is not infinite.
> > (W. F. Bolton, *The English Language*)

> Back in the Arts faculty, she replaced the original memo ... on Professor Bodgering's desk.
> > (Charles H. Cutting, *The Surleighwick Effect*)

> It [English] is frequently spoken, and almost universally understood, in Holland; it is kindly entertained as a relation in the most civilised parts of Germany; and it is studied as a learned language, though yet little spoke, by all those in France and Italy, who either have, or pretend to have, any learning.
> > (P. D. Stanhope, letter to *The World*, 28 November 1754)

Separators 3 *always* appear in pairs because they enclose a discrete piece of information. These two separators are brackets and quotation marks:

> The site extends to 424 sq. m. (or thereabouts) and is currently grassed.

> Intellectuals frequently show off by peppering their conversation with 'Japlish'.   (*Sunday Times*)

Virtually all users of language assume they know what a sentence is. We may not all be able to put this knowledge into words, but if we were presented with any passage of any language using the Roman alphabet and modern punctuation conventions, we would be able to count sentences. We can test this claim by looking at such a passage as the following:

> Bhí mise féin agus mo chara i nDúngeannain, Dia Luan seo chuaidh thart. Chonaic muid gasúr beag agus é ag siúl go gasta. 'C'é h-é sin?' adúirt mo chara. 'Níl fhios agam ar chor ar bith,' arsa mise.

We may not know the language from which this illustration is taken, but we can make a number of deductions. We can see that the passage involves direct speech as well as either narrative or reported speech, and that there are four sentences. We recognize words because, in the written medium, they have a space on either side and we recognize sentences because, again in the written medium, they begin with a capital letter and end with a full stop. Many linguists have struggled hard to define sentences. Around 100BC, Dionysius Thrax decided that a sentence contained a complete thought, but he did not reveal what an incomplete thought might be or how many thoughts and thus, perhaps, sentences might be involved in: 'I thought about it from every angle before I made up my mind.'

Modern linguists have offered hundreds of definitions of sentences, all of them valuable, none of them totally satisfactory. An American linguist, C. C. Fries, studied over 200 definitions of 'sentence' (see Chapter 2, *The Structure of English*, 1952) before deciding that one of the most useful was 'a stretch of language beginning with a capital letter and ending with a full stop'.

For our purposes, we shall subdivide sentences into different types, indicating which types of punctuation are appropriate. There are five main types of sentence, each of which can be either positive or negative:

1 **declarative sentences**, which make statements:
    Trees are green.
    I haven't seen them for weeks.
2 **imperative sentences**, which give orders:
    Come in.
    Don't let them pressurize you.
3 **exclamations:**
    You must have been crazy!
    You cannot be serious!
4 **questions:**
    Would you like some coffee?
    Isn't there any alternative?
5 **minor sentences**, which do not contain a main verb but which have the rhythm of sentences when spoken and the appropriate punctuation mark when written:
    One member one vote.
    No way, José!
    One lump or two?

Longer and more complex sentences still begin with a capital letter and end with a full stop, but they often use other punctuation marks, such as commas, to separate one part of the sentence from the rest. When writers wish to be precise about time, for example, they often begin or end a sentence with a clause relating to time that is separated from the rest of the sentence by means of a comma:

When I first arrived, I knew nobody.
I knew nobody, when I first arrived.

When they give an example, it is highlighted by being preceded and followed by commas:

If we choose an abstract noun, such as beauty, we can make certain claims about it.

Generally, long sentences need more punctuation marks than short ones, if they are to fulfil their purpose of guaranteeing clarity. The most frequently used punctuation marks within a sentence are commas, dashes, brackets, semicolons and colons, all of which are dealt with, in detail, in Section 2.

Sentences that deal with a related theme are usually grouped together into paragraphs. As with the term *sentence*, it is easier to pick out a paragraph than to define one. A paragraph is physically separated from other blocks of language by indentation or by spacing, but not by both. It should also have semantic coherence in that the sentences in it should be a step in the development of an argument, idea or narrative.

In traditional education, children were taught that each paragraph in an essay should have a *topic sentence*, that is, a sentence that contains the main idea of the paragraph. Paragraphs were then divided into three main types, depending on where the writer put the topic sentence. Sometimes, the topic sentence comes first, as in:

> A topic sentence is the most important sentence in a paragraph. It expresses the main idea that the paragraph wishes to convey. The other sentences in the paragraph tend to develop, modify, qualify or illustrate this central theme.

Sometimes, it comes in the middle of a paragraph, following one or more transitional sentences:

> A paragraph is usually composed of several sentences, linked by subject matter, vocabulary and tense. The topic sentence is the most important sentence in a paragraph. It expresses the main idea that the paragraph wishes to convey. The other sentences in the paragraph tend to develop, modify, qualify or illustrate this central theme.

The topic is the last sentence in a paragraph when a writer aims at what is called a *punchline*. This type of paragraph is often found in anecdotes and jokes, or when the writer wants to delay information:

> A paragraph is usually composed of several sentences, which are linked by subject matter, vocabulary and tense.

The sentences tend to develop, modify, qualify or illustrate a central theme, which is expressed most succinctly in one sentence. This is the topic sentence, the most important sentence in a paragraph.

Today's taste

Anyone who reads widely will be aware of two facts about contemporary punctuation, namely that punctuation in the past was much heavier than it is today and that personal computers have encouraged changes in punctuation preferences over the last quarter of a century.

An easy way to illustrate the first point is to juxtapose an extract from the King James's Bible (in modern spelling) with the same extract from a contemporary translation.

1 Behold my servant, whom I uphold; mine elect, in whom my soul delighteth; I have put my spirit upon him: he shall bring forth judgment to the Gentiles.
2 He shall not cry, nor lift up, nor cause his voice to be heard in the street.
3 A bruised reed shall he not break, and the smoking flax shall he not quench: he shall bring forth judgment unto truth.
4 He shall not fail nor be discouraged, till he have set judgment in the earth: and the isles shall wait for his law.

(Isaiah 42, verses 1–4)

The second version, which is set as if it were verse, comes from the Jersualem Mass Sheet, 9 January 1994:

Here is my servant whom I uphold,
my chosen one in whom my soul delights.
I have endowed him with my spirit
that he may bring true justice to the nations.

He does not cry out or shout aloud,
or make his voice heard in the streets.
He does not break the crushed reed,
nor quench the wavering flame.

Faithfully he brings true justice;
He will neither waver nor be crushed
until true justice is established on earth,
for the islands are awaiting his law.

A superficial examination shows three main changes between the earlier and the later version:

i   the older version uses more punctuation marks
ii   the older version uses a wider range of punctuation marks
iii the older version uses longer sentences.

A more thorough comparison of the versions reveals the following pattern:

Number of	KING JAMES	JERUSALEM
Punctuation marks	15	11
Full stops	4	5
Commas	6	5
Colons	3	0
Semicolons	2	1

It is debatable whether the modernization of the biblical punctuation is an improvement, or even desirable. Nevertheless, punctuation today tends to be simpler than it was in the past. Most writers tend to use shorter sentences and therefore more full stops, to use fewer colons, semicolons and dashes, and to avoid combined punctuation marks.

The differences that have been introduced by personal computers include the more frequent use of asterisks *, brackets of various shapes (), [], {}, and symbols such as ^, #, ~. Computers facilitate right-hand justification, giving users access to techniques that were once only found in professionally printed material.

The laws of punctuation are not, never have been, and never could be, irrevocably fixed. They are like the laws of the land, vitally important for freedom of expression, but, like the laws of the land, they can change in response to changing customs and advancing technology. In the fourteenth century, the virgule was among the most frequently used marks in writing. Today, the term is virtually unknown, except to people who have been exposed to French *dictée* (dictation) and learnt such instructions as *point* (full stop), *point virgule* (semicolon) and *virgule* (comma). To say that punctuation is not irrevocably fixed, however, is not to say that there is chaos. At any one time, we can specify what is correct and acceptable, but we cannot insist that the identical rules will apply in twenty-five years' time. In this book, we shall deal with the common core of punctuation and our examples will be taken from a wide range of literature, from broadsheet and from tabloid newspapers, from advertisements and from posters; from the sort of material that we all read regularly. We shall show that punctuation is not an unnecessary chore, dreamed up by educationists to make our lives miserable. It is a system that allows us to write, and to be read, with clarity. Furthermore, once learned, it is a skill like bicycle-riding, easy to pick up again.

Section 2

Dictionary

For ease of use, Section 2 is arranged in dictionary form. Where information is given in more than one entry, cross-references are provided.

Abbreviations

Abbreviations are not, in themselves, a part of the punctuation system, but it is important to know which punctuation marks to use with them. The word derives from Latin *abbreviare*, 'to make short', and is cognate with the word 'brief'. Abbreviations belong to five different categories:

1. Some abbreviations are made up of the initial capital letters of the words in a phrase:
    ANC African National Congress
    BBC British Broadcasting Corporation
    CIA Central Intelligence Agency.
   Some of these abbreviations become *acronyms*, that is, they are read as words rather than as a set of letters. When this happens, lower-case letters are sometimes used:
    IATA International Air Transport Association
    NATO North Atlantic Treaty Organization
    UNESCO/Unesco United Nations Educational, Scientific and Cultural Organization.
   Such abbreviations do not normally take full stops today, although these were widely used in the past.

2   Some abbreviations are a combination of capital and lower-case letters. In this category, we find titles:

   Dr Mary Brown
   Mrs Brown
   Mary Brown Jr

degrees:

   DLitt
   PhD

scientific names:

   Pb (lead)
   Li   (lithium)

and abbreviations of languages:

   Gk (Greek)
   Lat (Latin).

Until recently, many of these abbreviations were followed by full stops and there is still a tendency to use the punctuation mark in very formal styles:

   The degree ceremony was inaugurated by John Brown, D.Litt.

3   Some abbreviations involve the use of a single capital letter. This technique is used for names:

   J. B. Priestley
   J. M. Barrie

and for cardinal points:

   N   (north)
   S   (south)
   NE   (northeast)
   SSW (south by southwest).

Traditionally, these single-letter abbreviations each took a full stop. In Britain today there is a tendency to use them without the punctuation mark.

4   Some abbreviations use lower-case letters only:

   d diameter, old pence
   g gravity
   p penny, pence
   r radius.

This category includes many abbreviations from Latin, including:

e.g. (*exempli gratia*) for example

verb. sap. (*verbum sapienti sat est*) enough said (a word to the wise is sufficient)

5 Abbreviations for currency, weights and measures never take a full stop:

£12, 11p, $95, 6c

g, kg, lb, oz

ft, in, km, yd

There is a growing tendency for full stops to be omitted in abbreviations, except for those deriving from Latin or when the omission of full stops might cause confusion, as with *a.m.* being confused with *am*. Abbreviations used to be a common feature in personal letters, as is indicated by the first few lines of a letter from Winston Churchill to T. E. Lawrence (1927):

16.v.27   Treasury Chambers, Whitehall, sw

My dear 'Lurens'

I read with rapt attention the long letter you wrote to Eddie about my book. It is a poor thing, mainly a pot-boiler, & deriving a passing vogue from the tremendous events with wh it deals & the curiosity of the British public to know something about them. In fact, when I put down the Seven Pillars, I felt mortified at the contrast between my dictated journalism & yr grand & permanent contribution to English literature.

(A. W. Lawrence, *Letters to T. E. Lawrence*)

It is advisable to avoid abbreviations, especially in formal styles, unless they are necessary (e.g. the use of *Mrs*) and unlikely to be misunderstood.

Abbreviations take an article according to the pronunciation of the first letters used. Thus, *an LL.B*, *an MA*, *an MP*, but *a DLitt*, *a PM* and *a QC*. The two apparent exceptions to this rule are *a MS* and *a N. Ireland directive*. Both of these are pronounced as words, however, not letters. In other words, one tends to say *an MP* but *a manuscript*.

SEE ALSO: *full stop*

Accent marks

Accent marks are indicators to alert the reader that the marked words are pronounced differently. Accent marks, also sometimes referred to as diacritics, are used sparingly in English. They are limited to phonetics and to names and items adopted from other languages. Accent marks allow writers to be more precise about pronunciation and, in the British Isles, their use goes back over one thousand years. Early Christians adopted the Latin alphabet for their own languages but found that it was not adequate to their needs. Irish monks, for example, found that they had eighteen letters – a, b, c, d, e, f, g, h, i, l, m, n, o, p, r, s, t, u – to represent over fifty sounds. They introduced a dot over a consonant to indicate that the sound differed from an unmarked consonant. Since the dot could be misread and was hard to print, a technique developed of replacing the dot with 'h'. Evidence of this is still found in names such as *Callaghan* and *Gallagher*, where the 'g' followed by 'h' is pronounced differently from a 'g' on its own.

In English, the commonest accent marks are used in words and phrases borrowed from French. These include:

- the **acute accent** [´] as in *entrée*, 'the main course', *passé*, 'out of date'.
- the **cedilla** [ ] as in *façade*, 'front of building, artificial effect', *François*.
- the **modern circumflex** [ˆ] as in *fête*, 'feast, holiday', *tête à tête*, 'private conversation between two'.
- **dieresis** [¨] as in *Brontë*, *Haïti* and *naïve*.
- the **grave accent** [`] as in *à la mode*, 'according to the fashion, (*of desserts*) with ice cream' and in phrases based on *à la mode*, including the un-French *à la king*.

Other accent marks occur in English when words and names from other languages are written. These include:

- the **tilde** [~], especially in Spanish words such as *El Niño*, *señora*.
- the **umlaut** [¨] as in German *Köln* and *über*.

When borrowed words or phrases become integrated into English the accent mark tends to be dropped, as in *à Dieu* > *adieu*, *cliché* > *cliche*, *Haïti* (three syllables) > *Haiti* (two syllables) and *rôle* > *role*.

Accent marks are sometimes used in verse. A grave accent can indicate that a syllable, usually *-ed*, should be pronounced in order to create a regular metrical pattern:

> Friends, Romans, countrymen, lend me your ears;
> I come to bury Caesar, not to praise him.
> The evil that men do lives after them,
> The good is oft interrèd with their bones.   (*Julius Caesar*)

Accent marks are also used in some dictionaries to indicate where the main stress falls in a word. The *Collins English Dictionary*, for example, shows that *come-back* is pronounced (ˈkʌmˌbæk), that is, with primary stress on 'come' and secondary stress on 'back'. *Webster's Ninth New Collegiate Dictionary* illustrates the pronunciation of the same word as /ˈkəm-ˌbak/.

SEE ALSO: *acute accent, circumflex, dieresis, grave accent, tilde, umlaut*

Acute accent

The acute accent [́] as in *manqué*, 'unfulfilled':

> She was really a scientist manqué.

came into the language with the French words in which it occurred. The name *acute* occurs in writing in the fourteenth century and derives from Latin *acutus*, 'sharpened', itself deriving ultimately from *acus* (needle). The accent is used to indicate that the vowel over which it is placed is pronounced differently from the unaccented vowel. Thus, French distinguishes in writing between the sounds of 'e' in *rebord* (edge), *rébus* (riddle), *règne* (reign) and *rêver* (to dream). The accent is most frequently used to indicate a specific sound in French words but it occurs occasionally to represent the syllable with the strongest stress as in Spanish *hábil* (clever).

Often, anglicized versions of borrowed French words exist with meanings that are quite distinct from the accented forms. *Entry*, for example, was borrowed and adapted in the thirteenth century. Occasionally, the accents allow us to distinguish between words that would otherwise be identical in form, as with the verb *resume* and the noun *résumé*, 'summary', or with the verb *expose* and the noun *exposé*, 'revelation of facts'.

SEE ALSO: *accent marks*

Ampersand

The ampersand (&) is not, strictly speaking, a punctuation mark. Rather, it is a symbol, like $ or £. It was used in medieval manuscripts, carried over into printing and widely used in familiar writing as an abbreviation for 'and'. The name is a contraction of the expression *and per se and*, meaning 'and by itself [=] and'. Ampersand (&) was used by medieval monks as a stylized form of Latin *et*, 'and'. It is still quite widely used in business names:

Bradford & Bingley
Leeds & Holbeck
Marks & Spencer.

The use of *&c* for *etc.*, 'et cetera', is now extremely rare, although the practice was common until the end of the nineteenth century.

SEE ALSO: *abbreviations*

Angle brackets

Angle brackets ⟨ ⟩ tend to be restricted to works of scholarship and are therefore not appropriate in casual styles. They are used to supply text that is absent, defective, illegible or missing:

She by a sycamore,
Whose all-belated leaves yield up themselves

> To the often takings of desirous winds,
> Sits without consolation, marking not
> The time save when her tears which still ⟨descend⟩
> > (G. M. Hopkins, 'Stephen and Barberie')

> Poor soul, the centre of my sinful earth,
> ⟨Fool'd by⟩ these rebel powers that thee array
> > (Shakespeare, Sonnet cxlvi)

> The handwriting is not clear at this point. It may be: 'We ⟨can⟩ all try but ⟨we⟩ cannot all succeed.' It is possible, however, that it is: 'We ⟨must⟩ all try but ⟨we⟩ cannot all succeed.'

Angle brackets have special purposes in linguistics, such as the use of ⟨a⟩ to represent the letter 'a' in all its written forms. The single angle bracket [<] is used to mean 'develops from/has developed from':

> $I < Ic(c) = $ 'I' has developed from 'Ic' or 'Icc'.

The single angle bracket [>] is used to mean 'becomes/has become':

> $Ic(c) > I = $ 'Ic' and 'Icc' have become 'I'.

SEE ALSO: *brackets*

Apostrophe

The apostrophe is a separator. The word, derived from the Greek word *apostrophe*, meaning 'turning away', was first used in English in the sixteenth century, and is symbolized by [']. Shakespeare's schoolmaster character, Holofernes, in *Love's Labour's Lost*, uses the term, in an earlier form, in Act IV, Scene ii:

> You find not the apostrophas, and so miss the accent.

The apostrophe is currently used for the following eight purposes:

> to indicate possession in a noun or noun phrase:

Indra's sari
the baby's bottle
the Archbishop of Canterbury's address
China rejects the Governor Chris Patten's proposals (BBC
News at One).

The apostrophe precedes the 's' when the possessor is singular:

the child's toys
the people's choice = the choice of people

or when the plural noun is irregular and does not end in an 's':

the children's toys
the men's wages
the women's preoccupation.

The apostrophe follows the 's' when the possessor is a
regular plural noun:

the books' covers = the covers of the books
different peoples' cultures = the cultures of different
peoples.

Nouns that end in 'y' and that form their plural in 'ies' are
treated in the same way: the apostrophe follows the 's':

the babies' toys
the fillies' race.

to indicate time or quantity:

in two days' time
next year's timetable
their salary's value.

to indicate the omission of figures in dates:

'Who fears to speak of '98?' (song, referring to the 1798
rebellion in Ireland)
10th Dec. '94.

to indicate the omission of letters:

cannot → can't

Johannesburg → Jo'burg
of the clock → o'clock
we are → we're
will of the wisp → will o' the wisp

Your country is going down the plughole, and you can't spot it, 'cos you're still floating.

(*Sunday Times* Supplement)

In the past, *shan't* was written *sha'n't* to indicate that letters were omitted from both 'shall' and 'not'. Similarly, *influenza* became *'flu'*. Today, the forms *can't* and *won't*, like *shan't*, are written with one apostrophe. Well-known reductions, such as *flu* and *photo*, are usually written without apostrophes.

Sometimes the spelling of abbreviations is anglicized as the words and the things they represent become more familiar. Thus:

nuclear → nuke rather than *nuc'*
perambulator → pram rather than *peram'*
television → telly rather than *tele'*.

5 Apostrophes are also frequently employed to represent non-standard speech:

'T' maister's down i' t' fowld. Go round by th' end ot' laith, if ye went to spake to him.'

(Emily Brontë, *Wuthering Heights*)

This device is sometimes referred to as 'eye dialect' in that the density of apostrophes suggests that the passage is unusual in some way. Occasionally, a writer may suggest dialect by using *'n* to represent 'and'. Yet all speakers. and not just dialect speakers, use such a form in expressions like: *bread 'n butter*, *fish 'n chips* and *odds 'n ends*.

6 to represent Irish names:

Shane O'Neill had his headquarters in Dungannon.

This usage makes the Irish surname resemble such names as:

John o'Gaunt (John of Gaunt, i.e., Ghent, 1340–99)

John o'Groats (most northeasterly tip of the Scottish mainland).

In fact, the Irish *O* is not a reduction of *of* but an anglicization of *ua* meaning 'grandson, descendant'. Thus Shane O'Neill means 'John, Niall's grandson', and some Irish people insist on writing their names without the apostrophe, that is, in the form *Seán O Boyle*.

7 Apostrophes are sometimes also used to indicate the plural of numbers:

She was the best-known woman in the world in the 1980's.

abbreviations:

Laser PC's by VTech

and words being discussed as words:

Have you noticed how many we's he uses?
He provided a list of do's and don't's.

Many writers do not like the use of apostrophes in such cases, however, preferring with numbers and abbreviations to add the 's' only:

the 1980s
1700 JPs.

8 Occasionally, the apostrophe is used to indicate the plural of letters as in:

How many s's are there in Mississippi?
The i's usually come before the e's in English words.

Although this is acceptable, it looks odd and can therefore impede smooth reading. Singular forms of letters should be used if it is possible:

The spelling rule is i before e except after c.

The apostrophe should, however, be used if its omission would cause confusion:

The usual i's were replaced by Arabic numerals.

In order to avoid misusing the apostrophe, the following points should be borne in mind:

- *It's* always means 'it is'. Apostrophes are not needed with possessive adjectives:

    It's half past three.

    but:

    It has 'Russell' on its collar.

- *Who's* always means 'who is' and is not to be confused with 'whose':

    Who's the king of the castle?

    Whose book is that?

    These are the parents whose son broke the record.

- *There's* always means 'there is' and it tends to occur at the beginning of a sentence:

    There's a lot to be said for this point of view.

    The homophone 'theirs' should not be given an apostrophe:

    We had six entries but theirs is the best.

    I preferred hers but you liked theirs best.

    We can generalize about the last point and state that the possessive pronouns 'his', 'hers', 'ours', 'yours' and 'theirs' do not need an apostrophe.

- Singular names ending in 's' add an apostrophe + s to indicate possession:

    Keats's letters

    Yeats's poetic achievements.

    Some writers avoid using the apostrophe + s to indicate the possessive form of names which have more than one sibilant in the last syllable, preferring 'Jesus' followers' to 'Jesus's followers'.

    It is also customary to avoid using the apostrophe + s to form the possessive of classical names that end in 's'. Thus it is preferable to use:

    Achilles' heel not *Achilles's heel

    Archimedes' discovery not *Archimedes's discovery

    and:

    Euripides' plays not *Euripides's plays.

- The use of the apostrophe + s to form the plural of words ending in vowels is incorrect but widespread:

    *potato's (for potatoes)
    *radio's (for radios)
    *stereo's (for stereos)
    *tornado's (for tornadoes).

This practice may, however, derive from the custom of using an apostrophe + s to indicate the plural of non-English words such as *folio's* or *quarto's*. This usage was correct once, just as it was once considered correct to drink tea from a saucer.

- Problems with the apostrophe have existed for some time, if we judge by the non-occurrence of the apostrophe in placenames such as Gerrards Cross, St Andrews and St Chads.

    The apostrophe is, of course, normally used when the placename involves possession:

    Hunter's Quay
    Orme's Head
    St James's Street.

- Usually, we do not use an apostrophe when referring to shops:

    I'll meet you outside Kellys.

    and there is a tendency to use what sounds like a plural form ending in 's' even when the name does not contain one:

    Did you manage to get to Marks & Spencers?
    You can park under Morrisons.

    An apostrophe is used, however, when we use the title with a following noun:

    We'll meet outside Kelly's (or Kellys') pub.
    You can park under Morrison's (or Morrisons') supermarket.

- The rules for the use of the apostrophe with hyphenated plurals is worth emphasizing. Usually, we pluralize the most important element of the word, most often the first noun:

    brother-in-law, brothers-in-law
    My brothers-in-law are both married.

We indicate possession, however, by adding an ending to the last word in the compound:

My brother-in-law's motorbike is a Honda.

Both my brothers-in-law's motorbikes are Hondas.

This is similar to the use of an apostrophe + s after a phrase, as in the quotation from the back page of a tabloid newspaper:

The players on the field's opinion was not sought.

● There is some confusion among speakers about whether or not to use an apostrophe + s before a gerund (a noun formed from the present participle of the verb). Although the following sentences are both correct:

We talked about John's going.

We talked about John going.

the form using the apostrophe + s is regarded as more acceptable in formal contexts. Similarly, the sentence:

We talked about his going.

is more acceptable than its colloquial equivalent:

We talked about him going.

Winifred Nowottny once wrote that poetry was 'language at full stretch'. By this she meant that creative writers often exploit the potential of the language for literary effect. The apostrophe, too, has been used in this way by James Joyce in *Finnegans Wake*. The title, without an apostrophe, is a visual reminder that normal rules of language will not apply and they don't. The novel begins, apparently in mid-sentence:

riverrun, past Eve and Adam's, from swerve of shore to bend of bay, brings us by a commodius vicus of recirculation back to Howth Castle and Environs.

The first part of the sentence is not provided until the end of the book:

Till thousendsthee. Lps. The key to. Given! A way a lone a last a loved a long the

SEE ALSO: *contractions*

Asterisk

The word *asterisk* comes from the Greek word *asteriskos*, 'little star'. It was first used in English in 1382 by Wyclif in the form *asterichos*. It is symbolized by [*] and is currently used for six main purposes:

1   To indicate the omission of letters in so-called 'taboo vocabulary':

> The BBC does not officially permit the use of even mild swear words such as bl**dy before 9 pm.

> P*** off or I'll call the police.   (*Sun* headline)

2   to refer to a note or a reference, given at the bottom of the same page. This usually occurs when there is only one note or reference. The asterisk follows the word or structure that is being annotated:

> This is the first television showing of Scarlet and Black.*

It precedes the explanation at the bottom of the page:

> *The title of this BBC series is based on Stendhal's novel *Le Rouge et le Noir*.

In contemporary usage, superscript numbers are preferred in texts to asterisks. If an asterisk is used, however, it resembles a footnote number in being placed slightly above the line and always following the punctuation marks, if there are any.

3   to mark a cross-reference in a dictionary or an encyclopedia. The asterisk may precede or follow the item as in:

> *Tense

> Tense*

both meaning: There is a separate entry under 'Tense'.

4   In stories, a line of asterisks is occasionally used to indicate that a period of time has passed.

5   to denote a hypothetical or unattested form in historical linguistics:

> Modern 'day' derives from O.E. 'dæg'. It is cognate with Gothic 'dags' and Indo-European *dhoghos.

Such reconstructed words are often referred to as 'starred forms'.

6   to designate an unacceptable word or structure in contemporary linguistics:

　　*brickable

　　*I be not happy.

Sometimes, when the form is marginally acceptable, the asterisk is preceded by a question mark:

　　?*runnable

　　?*I may have been being bullied.

SEE ALSO: *footnote*

Bar

A bar is a separator. It is an alternative term for the diagonal mark (/), also known as a *diagonal*, *oblique mark*, *slash*, *solidus* and *virgule*. In spite of the proliferation of terms, this punctuation mark is not used frequently, but occurs mainly:

● to separate alternatives:

　　and/or

　　he/she

　　A good writer will learn from, but not be limited to, her/his own experiences.

● to indicate the end of poetic lines when verse is quoted as if it were prose:

　　He led his regiment from behind/He found it less exciting.

　　　　　　　　　　　　　(W. S. Gilbert, *The Gondoliers*)

　　Unless space is at a premium, quotations from poetry should be set out as verse.

● to mark phonemes:

　　The /l/ sounds in the words leap and peel are pronounced very differently in many dialects of English.

　　　　　　　　　　　(David Crystal, *Linguistics*, p. 179)

● to imply 'per' in abbreviations:

　　Wages: £4.85/hr.

● occasionally to separate years:

　　This demand relates to the 1994/95 tax year.

　　and also days, months and years in dates:

Date of birth: 19/11/72.

In many parts of the world, including the United States of America, the month comes first:

Date of birth: 11/19/72.

In order to avoid ambiguity, some people use Arabic numerals for the day and Roman numerals for the month:

Date of birth: 19/xi/72.

SEE ALSO: *diagonal, oblique mark, slash, solidus, virgule*

Brace brackets

Because of their shape, brace brackets { } are also known as 'curly brackets'. They are most widely used to enclose alternatives. The alternatives may be letters:

There are many words in the language which end in the sequence -in. All of the following are acceptable:

$$\left\{ \begin{array}{c} b \\ ch \\ d \\ g \\ gr \end{array} \right\} + in$$

or sounds:

The words 'bin', 'tin', 'kin' are acceptable:

$$\left\{ \begin{array}{c} b \\ t \\ k \end{array} \right\} + in$$

or affixes:

The prefixes 'con-', 'de-', 'in-' and 're-' can all occur in noun sets, such as:

$$\left\{ \begin{array}{c} con \\ de \\ in \\ re \end{array} \right\} + ception$$

or words or phrases:

He is coming $\begin{Bmatrix} \text{too.} \\ \text{as well} \end{Bmatrix}$

Occasionally, only one brace bracket is used:

degrees $\left\{ \begin{array}{l} \text{BA} \\ \text{MA} \\ \text{PhD} \end{array} \right.$

SEE ALSO: *brackets*

Brackets

Brackets are separators. The word *bracket* is one of the few punctuation words in English not derived from Greek or Latin. It is a Germanic word, coming from the same root as *brace* and *breeches*. The term was originally used in English to refer to stone, wood or metal projecting from a wall. By 1750. the word was applied to a pair of marks used in writing or printing to enclose a piece of material. Today there are four main types of bracket: angle brackets $\langle \rangle$, brace brackets $\{ \}$, round brackets () and square brackets [].

- In works on the English language, **angle** brackets are used to supply text that is either absent, defective, illegible or missing and for specialized uses in linguistics.
- **Brace** brackets are used to enclose alternatives.
- **Round** brackets are currently the most widely used type of brackets. They are also called *parentheses* (singular *parenthesis*) because the information they enclose is parenthetic. that is, explanatory, optional or supplementary.
- **Square** brackets are used mainly for parentheses within parentheses, to indicate that a quoted form is accurately quoted but not quite right, and to enclose phonetic symbols.

SEE ALSO: *angle brackets, brace brackets, parentheses, round brackets, square brackets*

Capitalization

In the past, capital letters were often used, as in German, for nouns, especially abstract nouns:

> I have brought Philosophy out of Closets and Libraries, Schools and Colleges, to dwell in Clubs and Assemblies, at Tea-Tables and in Coffee-Houses.
>
> (Joseph Addison, *Spectator*, No. 10, 1711)

The name *capital* is derived from Latin *capitalis*, meaning 'head, foremost'. It was applied in the fourteenth century to letters that appeared at the beginning or head of a text. In written English, two types of letters are used. The A, B, C set is referred to as capital letters, or upper-case letters or majuscules. The a, b, c set is referred to as small letters, lower-case letters or minuscules. The technique of using capital letters for the first word in a sentence began to be widely used in England in the thirteenth century although it was not consistently applied until the end of the sixteenth century. The technique of using capital letters in this way is widely but not universally applied. Arabic, for example, does not use it.

Initial capital letters are used for many purposes in English. For ease of reference, we have divided these into ten main categories.

- First words
- Exclamations
- Pronouns and possessive adjectives
- Proper nouns
- Historical and archaeological periods and events
- Names of vehicles and products
- Book titles, works of art, major pieces of music, newspapers, magazines, films, and TV and radio programmes
- Abbreviations and acronyms
- Scientific terms
- Parliamentary acts and bills.

First words

Capital letters indicate the first word in a sentence or sentence fragment:

> I'm going to get married.
> Well!
> At Christmas.
> Splendid.
> To Athene.
> Who?   (Brian Friel's play, *Translations*)

The rule applies also to the first word of greeting in a letter:

> Dear Ms Jones
> My dear Michael

to postcodes:

> Leeds LS2 9JT

to postscripts:

> PS   I love you.

and to the first word in a direct quotation:

> Schneider added, 'Normality is boring, whereas dysfunctionality is interesting.'   (*Sunday Times*)

The first word in a line of poetry is also marked by the use of a capital letter:

> Grief, grief, I suppose and sufficient
> Grief makes us free
> To be faithless and faithful together
> As we have to be.   (D. H. Lawrence, 'Hymn to Priapus')

Occasionally, especially in contemporary poetry, writers make use of verse paragraphs, using capital letters as we do in prose:

> *O* was the conch-shell's invocation, *mer* was
> both mother and sea in our Antillean patois,
> *os*, a grey bone, and the white surf as it crashes

and spreads its sibilant collar on the lace shore.

(Derek Walcott, *Omeros*)

and some, following the example of e. e. cummings, use lower-case letters for their names and use punctuation marks idio-syncratically:

> my sweet old etcetera
> aunt lucy during the recent
> war could and what is more did tell you just
> what everybody was fighting
>
> for

(e. e. cummings, 'my sweet old etcetera')

In poetry, too, capital letters were sometimes used, when a noun, usually an abstract noun, was being personified:

> Can Honour's voice provoke the silent dust,
> Or Flatt'ry soothe the dull cold ear of Death?
> (Thomas Gray, 'Elegy Written in a Country Churchyard')

Exclamations

The first word in an exclamation takes a capital letter:

> Wow! My word!

'O' is always capitalized:

> O my goodness and O my goodness gracious!

'Oh' is capitalized only at the beginning of an utterance:

> Oh my goodness and oh my goodness gracious!

Pronouns and possessive adjectives

In English, the first person singular pronoun *I* is always capitalized:

> If I were a blackbird, I'd whistle and sing,
> I'd follow the ship that my true love sails in.

Capital letters continue to be used for pronouns and possessive adjectives associated with God and some saints:

> Our Lord
> Our Lady
> The Lord spoke to the multitude and He said ...
> Our Father Who art in heaven, hallowed be Thy name.

In certain formal circumstances, capital letters are used for possessive adjectives that refer to the sovereign or to a high-ranking dignitary:

> Her Majesty, the Queen
> His Excellency.

In the past, it was also common for capital letters to be used for pronouns referring to the sovereign:

> When Queen Elizabeth I went on a royal progress in 1570, She was attended by sixteen ladies-in-waiting.

This is no longer widespread, lower-case letters now being preferred:

> When Queen Elizabeth II spoke recently, she described her *annus horribilis*.

It is still usual, however, for titles of courtesy, honour or respect to be capitalized:

> HRH, the Prince of Wales
> His Grace, the Bishop of London.

Proper nouns

Capital letters are used for proper nouns and for the words closely associated with them. We use them for people's surnames and given names, whether in full or as initials:

> Jack Horner
> Barbara M. H. Strang

for nicknames:

> the Iron Lady
> the Teflon Man

and for many words derived from proper names:

> Americanize
> Thatcherism.

The rule here is simple. When a proper noun is adopted and adapted, it keeps its capital letter as long as it is associated with a person or place. When the association weakens, there is a tendency to use a lower-case letter:

> Bowdler > bowdlerize
> Boycott > boycott.

We also use capital letters for titles that precede a person's name:

> King George V
> President Clinton
> Professor Baxter

but:

> George V, the bearded king of England
> the tenth president of the United States
> six university professors.

Hyphenated titles are capitalized in both parts:

> Major-General Moore
> Vice-President Gore.

Capital letters are conventionally used for religious titles such as:

> the Prophet Muhammad
> the Blessed Trinity
> the Blessed Virgin
> the Holy Spirit

and for religious denominations:

> Nonconformist
> Russian Orthodox.

Capital letters are also used for the days of the week:

> Monday's child is fair of face

for important holidays and festivals:

> August Bank Holiday
> Christmas Day
> Easter
> May Day
> Passover
> Ramadan

and for the months of the year:

> Thirty days hath September,
> April, June and November.

Capital letters are not normally used for the names of the seasons:

> She wears her summer nighties in the summer when it's hot.
> She wears her winter woollies in the winter when it's not.
>> (Traditional song)

The names of countries are also written with capital letters:

> Algeria
> Canada
> Papua New Guinea

as are the names of languages:

> Arabic
> Hopi
> Japanese

and the names of the inhabitants of a country:

> Egyptian(s)
> Israeli(s)
> Mongolian(s).

English differs from most other European languages in using capital letters for adjectives derived from proper names:

a French lady *but* une dame française
a Spanish book *but* un livre espagnol
European languages *but* des langues européennes.

Capital letters are used for placenames, whether of cities, towns, villages or regions:

Port Harcourt
Harrogate
Tullyhogue
the Yorkshire Dales.

There is some vacillation in the use of capitals for food items involving placenames. Most writers use capitals to refer to:

Bath buns
Wensleydale cheese

but some use lower-case letters for:

brussels sprout
cheddar cheese.

In general, the capital should be preserved when there is still some link with the place of origin. For example, people rarely associate the vegetable with the capital of Belgium.

Capital letters are also used for the names of houses, avenues, roads, groves, hills, parks, terraces, streets and other similar designations when they occur with a name:

'Seaview'
12 Beach Avenue
Beach Road

for the names of specific rivers, mountains, major geographical features and geological formations:

the River Rhine
Mount Kilimanjaro
Lake Windermere
the Grand Canyon

but these nouns are not capitalized when they are used non-specifically:

the rivers of Germany
the mountains of East Africa
the lakes of Britain
a series of canyons.

Capital letters are used for the compass points:

NNW = North North West
SE = South East
The North.

The words North, South, East and West are capitalized when they occur as part of a geographical region:

East Anglia
North Africa
South America
West Wales.

Capital letters are used for organizations, both religious and secular:

Christianity
Marxism
the Crown
the Senate
Department for Education
British Gas
the *Observer*
The Times
Morrisons.

There is usually no apostrophe in shop names unless the name is followed by a term such as 'supermarket':

Morrisons' supermarket.

Historical and archaeological periods and events

Capital letters are used in the designation of significant eras and episodes:

> the Neolithic Period
> the Renaissance
> the Glorious Revolution
> the Six Days' War.

Names of vehicles and products

The names of land, air, sea and space vehicles take capital letters:

> *The Flying Scotsman*
> *The Spirit of St Louis*
> the *Titanic*
> the *Hotol*.

In general, the article is given a capital letter when it is an integral part of the name.

The names of vehicle types are also capitalized:

> a Dormobile
> a Jaguar
> a Vitara

as are brandnames:

> an Electrolux
> a Guinness
> Coca Cola.

When a brandname is used to designate a group of similar products from different manufacturers, the initial capital is lost and the word can even change its class. Thus, 'Hoover' originally referred to a specific vacuum cleaner. Gradually, the term was applied to many types of vacuum cleaner and the word was written 'hoover':

> I need to buy a new hoover.
> Have you hoovered the stairs?

Book titles, works of art, major pieces of music, newspapers, magazines, films, and TV and radio programmes

Capital letters are used for the names of printed works and for forms of art and entertainment:

Modern Englishes
The Laughing Cavalier
Schubert's *Trout* piano quintet
the *Independent*
Sunday Times
Woman's Own
Gone with the Wind
After Henry.

Recently, some journals have begun to use lower-case letters for all the words in a book title except the first and those that, like the name of a language, must be capitalized:

A critical history of contemporary fiction
A grammar of contemporary English.

More usual and, at the moment, more acceptable is the use of capital letters for the first word and all the principal words in the title, that is, all words except articles (e.g. *the*), prepositions (e.g. *in*) and conjunctions (e.g. *and*):

A Critical History of Contemporary Fiction
A Grammar of Contemporary English.

Consistency is the most important criterion here. If the former style is selected, it must be adhered to systematically.

Capital letters, without italics, are preferred for religious writings such as:

the Bhagavad Gita
the Bible
the Pentateuch
the Koran

and for books of the Bible:

Genesis
Exodus.

Adjectives deriving from Bible, Gospel and Scripture are not capitalized:

a biblical story
the gospel truth
scriptural exegesis.

Abbreviations and acronyms

Most abbreviations and acronyms take capital letters for all their letters:

ASH (Action on Smoking and Health)
the BBC (British Broadcasting Corporation)
the TUC (Trades Union Congress).

Well-established publishing houses in Britain often use initials:

CUP (Cambridge University Press)
EUP (Edinburgh University Press)
OUP (Oxford University Press).

When Routledge was Routledge & Kegan Paul, it was referred to as RKP.

In British English, it is usual to write placename abbreviations, such as UK and USA, without full stops. Many Americans prefer to write U.K. and U.S.A.

Scientific terms

The names of scientific disciplines are normally capitalized:

Chemistry
Human Biology
Organic Chemistry
Physics.

There is a tendency for these terms to be written with lower-case initials in informal writing and when the meaning is not strictly scientific:

> the anatomy of the beetle
> sexual chemistry.

Capital letters are also used for the initial letter in chemical symbols:

> CO (carbon monoxide)
> Cu (copper)
> K (potassium)
> S (sulphur)

and for the names of significant astronomical features:

> Jupiter
> the Milky Way
> the Orion Nebula.

Parliamentary acts and bills

These are capitalized but not italicized:

> the Act of Succession
> the Bill of Rights.

> SEE ALSO: *abbreviations, sentence*

Caret

A caret (∧) is used to indicate that an omission has occurred in writing, typing or printing. The word comes from Latin *caret* meaning 'there is missing'. The omitted word or phrase is usually written over the omission as in:

> 9:30
> I missed the ∧ train.

Cedilla

The cedilla [˛] is a mark like a comma that is placed under a 'c', usually before an 'o' or a 'u', to indicate that the 'c' is pronounced like the 'c' in 'cite' and not like the 'c' in 'caution'. The term dates from the sixteenth century and comes from Spanish *ceda* (zed) + *illa* (little), the word *ceda* deriving ultimately from Latin *zeta*. Originally, the Spanish used a small 'z' after the 'c' to indicate that the pronunciation of the 'c' had been modified. The cedilla is used most frequently in the representation of words from French and Portuguese. The same symbol is used under 's' in Turkish to indicate that the sound is to be pronounced 'sh'.

SEE ALSO: *accent marks*

Circumflex

The circumflex [^] is placed over a vowel to indicate that the pronunciation of the vowel differs from that of its unaccented counterpart. The word *circumflex* derives from Latin *circum* + *flectere* (to bend around) and was adopted into English in the sixteenth century. This accent, when used over words deriving from French, indicates a lengthening of the vowel, sometimes due to the loss of another sound. There is, for example, a correlation between some French words using ê and English words using e(a)s:

English	French	Latin
beast	bête	bestia
feast	fête	festa
vestment	vêtement	vestimentum

SEE ALSO: *accent marks*

Colon

The colon is a separator. The word was adopted into English in the sixteenth century and used by Puttenham in 1589:

> The auncient reformers of language, invented, three manner of pauses. The second they called colon ...
>
> (*English Poesie*, II, iv)

It comes from the Greek word *kolon*, meaning 'part of a stanza'. It is symbolized by [:] and is used for seven main purposes:

1 to separate a list from the main clause:
   You should always take a good supply of toiletries: soap, toothpaste, mouthwash, hand creams and deodorants.
2 to separate main clauses when the second seems to be an illustration of the first:
   The house looked sad and uncared for: it had been empty for two years.

Modern writers are more likely to use a dash, a semicolon or a full stop than a colon in such cases. Very careful writers, however, use a colon to link sentences when the second illustrates or expands the first:
   There was no love in his life: he felt utterly alone.

They use a semicolon to link parallel sentences:
   There was no love in his life; there was no-one to miss him.

and they use a full stop when the second sentence is semantically distinct from the first:
   There was no love in his life. He was, however, happy in his job.

3 to introduce examples or illustrations:
   Remember what he told us: Fool me once – shame on you. Fool me twice – shame on me.
4 to introduce quotations:
   Advertisements are often simple in structure: 'Think once. Think twice. Think bike.'
5 in writing the time:
   It is 9:26.
   Don't leave before 16:30.
6 in headlines, both to economize on space and to make a dramatic juxtaposition:
   Dead on the roof: the king of cocaine
                                        (*Sunday Times* headline)
7 between the title and subtitle of a book:
   Modern Englishes: Pidgins and Creoles
   Edith Sitwell: A Critical Essay.

Comma

The comma is a separator and is the most frequently used punctuation mark in the language. The word *comma* was first recorded in English in 1554. It derives ultimately from Greek *komma*, meaning 'clause, segment of sentence'. In English the comma is represented by a full stop with a tail [,]. It is used for nine main purposes:

Lists

Commas are used to separate items in lists of words, phrases or clauses:

> a happy, pleasant-looking individual
> They arrived with milk, sugar, butter, cheese and eggs.
> We searched in the desk, in the drawers, in the files and in the dustbin.
> I told them that I had bought the computer, put it on the back seat, locked the car and gone straight home.

In Britain, we do not normally use a comma between the last two items in a list if they are joined by a conjunction. Thus, the next two sentences are correct in both Britain and the United States of America:

> I want blue, green, yellow, black.
> I want blue, green, yellow and black.

However, the third usage, sometimes known as the 'Oxford' or 'serial comma', is today more widely acceptable in the United States of America or in areas influenced by American English:

> I want blue, green, yellow, and black.

However, a comma is used to avoid ambiguity when the last item in a list contains 'and':

> My father liked all comedians, especially Chaplin, Keaton, and Morecambe and Wise.
> Many large building societies are named after places: Leeds

and Holbeck, Cheltenham and Gloucester, and Bradford and Bingley.

Introductory clauses

Introductory clauses are separated from the rest of the sentence by a comma:

> When the fields are left fallow, wild flowers soon return to an area.
> If you don't follow the rules, it won't work.

Such clauses usually tell us when, where, how or why the main action occurred.

Reduced clauses are also separated from the rest of the sentence. These clauses generally contain either the infinitive (e.g. *to go*), the present participle (e.g. *wrapping*) or the past participle (e.g. *seen*):

> To settle his nerves, he drank a cup of hot, sweet tea.
> Wrapping the quilt round her, she fell fast asleep.
> Seen from here, the spire looks crooked.

Occasionally this use of the comma can prevent ambiguity:

> Walking on, his son, Robert, encountered a dragon.

In fairy tales, it is perhaps just conceivable that this sentence could be:

> Walking on his son, Robert encountered a dragon.

Foregrounding

Commas are used when part of a sentence is foregrounded. The foregrounding can highlight or emphasize information:

> Weary but happy, he felt.
> On a hill craggy and steep, truth stands.
> For five pounds, you sold it?

Separating

Commas are used to mark the boundaries of an insertion into a sentence. The insertion may be a word:

> I said, however, that I would be willing to make an exception.
> Will you take this, Mary, and give it to your mother.

or a phrase:

> He was, in fact, the man I had met earlier.

or a clause:

> He said, if I remember correctly, that he would return tomorrow at noon.

We should note that commas, like brackets, are used both before and after these insertions.

Indicating apposition

A noun phrase that is composed of a proper noun and a designation has the two parts separated by a comma:

> Mrs Bunn, the baker's wife
> John Smith, the renowned centre forward.

This type of structure is often called *noun phrases in apposition*. If such a structure occurs in a sentence, then commas are used before and after the explanatory phrase:

> Mrs Bunn, the baker's wife, was renowned for her short-crust pastry.

Non-defining clauses

Non-defining (non-restrictive) clauses are separated from the rest of the sentence:

> The passengers, who wore seatbelts, escaped unhurt.
> My friend, who writes poetry, lives in Wales now.

The houses, which have been renovated, are selling well.

A non-defining clause expands the noun it modifies, whereas a defining clause limits or reduces its application. Thus, in:

The passengers, who wore seatbelts, escaped unhurt.

we can delete the non-defining clause and make the correct deduction that:

The passengers (that is, all of them) escaped unhurt.

The sentence with a defining clause, in which commas are not used, limits the reference of the noun *passengers*. Thus, in the sentence:

The passengers who wore seatbelts escaped unhurt.

the relative clause is essential to our understanding that only *some* of the passengers escaped unhurt. The use or non-use of commas in such sentences is an integral part of the meaning.

Occasionally, non-defining relative clauses are marked off by dashes:

The passengers – who wore seatbelts – escaped unhurt.

In speech, non-defining clauses are signalled by pauses and a change of tone.

Main clauses

Compound sentences often need commas to separate long main clauses linked by *and, but* and *so*:

I've contacted your parents in Australia, and they will fly home on the first available plane.
We drove for hours and hours in the country, but still managed to be early for our appointment.
He couldn't eat any more food in the restaurant, so I asked for a doggy bag.

Many writers prefer to omit these commas. Commas are not used when the linked units are short:

He turned and left.

Dates and numbers

Commas are sometimes used to separate the year from the month:

13 November, 1995
It was in November, 1995, that we met.

Increasingly, as part of the movement away from heavy punctuation, the commas before and after the year are omitted:

It was in November 1995 that we met.

They are also employed to separate digits in long numbers:

135,265
1,987,456

Traditionally, the comma has been used, as above, to mark off thousands and millions. This convention continues to be applied, except with one thousand, which tends to be written 1000, or even 1 000, and not 1,000.

Correspondence

The salutation is often separated from the body of a letter:

Dear Michael,
I was very glad ...

(The conventions associated with punctuating a letter are dealt with in Section 3.)

Because commas are widely used, they are also widely misused. The following points should be helpful:

- Do not use a comma to end a sentence.
- Do not use a comma before the opening of parentheses, whether brackets or dashes.
- Do not introduce more commas than are absolutely necessary to express yourself with clarity.

- Commas can be used after sentence-initiating adverbials such as *however, indeed, meanwhile, nevertheless, no, yes*:

    Indeed, as I said before, there was no way of knowing how many people would come.

SEE ALSO: *brackets, dashes, numbers*

Compounding

One of the commonest methods of word formation in English is by means of combining two or three words to form a new one:

    all + be + it > albeit
    all + ready > already.

Sometimes the compound is written as separate words:

    red gum
    table tennis

sometimes hyphenated:

    red-hot
    table-ware

and sometimes as a single word:

    redwood
    tablespoon.

There are no totally fixed rules about the use of hyphens in compounds and dictionaries can differ in their treatment. The following guidelines may be helpful:

- If the compound has been in use for a considerable period, it is unlikely to be hyphenated:

    doorway
    handkerchief
    redbreast
    Whitehouse.

    Indeed, some well-established compounds are no longer thought of as compounds:

    altogether

childhood
eyebrow
lipstick
teenager.

● If the meaning of the compound is significantly different from the normal meanings of the combined words, the compound is unlikely to be hyphenated:

A black bird need not be a blackbird.

A greenhouse need not be green.

SEE ALSO: *hyphen*

Contractions

Contracted forms use the apostrophe to indicate the omission of one or more letters. Contractions are written as one word and the commonest in the language are the following:

● verb + not
are not > aren't
cannot > can't
could not > couldn't
dare not > daren't
did not > didn't
do not > don't

● pronoun + verb:
I am > I'm
you are > you're
he is/has > he's
she is/has > she's
we would > we'd
they will > they'll.

It is rare for two contractions to occur together, so:

he isn't

occurs rather than:

*he'sn't.

Contractions should be avoided in formal writing.

SEE ALSO: *abbreviations, apostrophe*

Dagger

This character, which is also sometimes called an *obelisk*, is shaped like a dagger. Textual references to its use in printing date from 1706. It was sometimes used to indicate the date of someone's death or to mark a reference, usually to a footnote. It is represented by (†).

Lauder, William (†1771)

The Latter-day Saints† are also known as Mormons.

† A religious community founded in the United States in 1830.

Since the advent of personal computers, superscript numbers have usually been preferred for footnote references, and the association with the date of death is obsolete.

A double dagger (‡), which is shaped at both ends like the hilt of a dagger, was also occasionally used to indicate a footnote.

In older books, the asterisk is sometimes used to indicate the first footnote, the dagger the second footnote, and the double dagger the third. Such usage is now obsolete.

SEE ALSO: *footnote*

Dash

The dash is a separator. The noun 'dash' had acquired the meaning of a hasty stroke of the pen by 1615:

And thus by meere chaunce with a little dash I have drawne the picture of a Pigmey.   (Jan Stephens, *Satirycall Essayes*)

By this time, it had also acquired the meaning of a mark used in writing to indicate a fault. By the early eighteenth century, it had come to refer to the punctuation mark, which we represent by [–]. The word 'dash' derives from a Middle English verb *dasshen*, first recorded in the fourteenth century and meaning 'knock, hurl, break'. The dash, partly through word association with 'slapdash', is often criticized as indicating carelessness, and it is undoubtedly overused by people who are not always clear about the rules of punctuation. Nevertheless, it has several legitimate uses in contemporary English and it would be a loss if, through ignorance or uncertainty, it was avoided altogether.

The dash is not found on the standard keyboard and this fact has encouraged people to substitute one or two hyphens (--) for it. In printing, there are two types of dash, an *em* dash, which is the width of the letter 'm', and an *en* dash, which is the width of the letter 'n'. The **em** rule or dash can be used:

- as a stylistic alternative to parentheses (brackets) or commas:

  When one does not know whether one's life is a tragedy or a comedy, the only *frisson* possible is that of despair – as Hugh, the enervate, hands over the baton of hope to Maire, the energised.

  (Richard Pine, *Brian Friel and Ireland's Drama*)

  Without these small pieces of evidence, easily missed – Emma does not notice them – one might conclude that the whole evening goes by without a sign of their acquaintance with each other.

  (Douglas Jefferson, *Jane Austen's* Emma)

  When the parenthetical comment occurs in the middle of a sentence, there are always two dashes:

  Prince Edward said: 'We are not planning to get married – we only met each other in the last few months – but we are good friends.'   (*Guardian*)
- to indicate an explanation or an expansion:

  We are conscious of literary experiences which appear to transcend language – plot, character, personality.
- to emphasize a point:

  Two surprises were new taxes on air travel, £5 on flights to Europe and £10 elsewhere – a blow for holidaymakers.

  (*Sunday Times*)

> Here, under leave of Brutus and the rest—
> For Brutus is an honourable man;
> So are they all, all honourable men—
> Come I to speak in Caesar's funeral.

(Julius Caesar)

- to indicate disjointed or unfinished speech or thoughts in fiction:

  > "Does he – does he – think – what does he think! Tell him – tell him –"   (Mark Twain, *Tom Sawyer Detective*)

  Often, foreign speech is marked in this way:

  > Ah, mine goot captain, mine very tear friend–vat–vat–vat av you done wid de cask captain?

  (Michael Scott, *Tom Cringle's Log*)

- as a shorthand device in journalism:

  > Electronic motorway tolls – when technology ready £10 billion chopped – details page 29   *(Sun)*
  > Taxpayer 'ripped off' – Labour   (Ceefax)

- to show that letters have been omitted:

  > Or perhaps he was incapable of articulate generalship: 'F--ing come ON! F--! Come f--ing on!' is the managerial line at big matches.   (*Sunday Times*)

- to indicate a dramatic pause:

  > The *Mary Celeste* was found – empty. Not a man, not an animal, not an insect was on board!

Fiction writers have, occasionally, used the dash to introduce direct speech. In James Joyce's *A Portrait of the Artist as a Young Man*, for example, we find such exchanges as:

> He poked one of the boys in the side with his pandybat, saying:
> – You, boy! When will Father Dolan be in again?
> – Tomorrow, sir, said Tom Furlong's voice.

In contemporary writing, the dash is seldom combined with another punctuation mark such as a comma or a question mark, although such combinations were popular in the past:

> Mrs. Elton had most kindly sent Jane a note, or we should
> have been. – But two such offers in one day! – Never were
> such neighbours. I said to my mother, 'Upon my word,
> ma'am –'.
> (Jane Austen, Emma)

It is still occasionally combined with a colon when a quotation is
introduced:

> My favourite two lines are:–
> Poets themselves must fall, like those they sung,
> Deaf the praised ear, and mute the tuneful tongue.

although most writers now use a colon on its own.

In printed material, the **en** dash or en rule is used for three main
purposes:

- for page references:
  > See pp. 16–23.

  Where several digits occur in the number, the last two are
  usually quoted:
  > 234–38

  although different publishers have different styles.
- to indicate 'up to and including':
  > 1939–45.

  Even when the numbers belong to the same decade, it is
  conventional to give the last two numbers:
  > 1931–39

  and not:
  > *1931–9.

  Where there is a change of century, the years are given in
  full:
  > 1890–1903.
- to compound proper nouns used adjectivally:
  > the Leeds–London train
  > the Bruno–Lewis fight.

  There is a semantic distinction between:
  > the Bruno–Lewis fight (with an en dash)
  where two people are involved, and:

the Windsor-Lewis collection (with a hyphen)

where the reference is to one individual with a double-barrelled name.

In practice, few people outside the world of publishing distinguish between the en rule and the hyphen. The en and the hyphen are both used for compounding and using the hyphen symbol for both causes no problem whatsoever. The dash or em rule is, however, different. It is used to separate parts of a sentence, not to link them. In the past, the dash did not have a space on either side of it:

Your question–if it was a question–is most unwelcome.

and some printers continue this practice. Many contemporary newspaper printers, however, use an en rule with a space on either side for a dash:

Your question – if it was a question – is most unwelcome.

SEE ALSO: *parentheses*

Diagonal

The term *diagonal* is occasionally used for [/], the punctuation mark that is also known as the *oblique mark, slash, solidus* or *virgule*.

SEE ALSO: *bar, oblique mark, slash, solidus, virgule*

Dieresis

Dieresis [¨] is occasionally spelt diaeresis. The word derives ultimately from Greek *diairesis*, meaning 'division', and it was adopted into English in the seventeenth century. It is placed on the second of two adjacent vowels to indicate that they are pronounced separately, as in *naïve*, rather than as a diphthong, as in *main*. The use of dieresis when two vowels co-occur because of a prefix, as in *coöccur*, is no longer current.

The dieresis is best known in English because of its use in the surname of the Brontës. It is unlikely that the sisters would have been any less literary if they had used a different form of their father's name, Prunty (also Brunty), but the continental appearance of Brontë lends an element of mystery to their background.

SEE ALSO: *accent marks*

Ditto

Ditto, or ditto marks, (,,) or (..), have been used in English since the seventeenth century. The term comes from the Tuscan dialect of Italian and means *said*. In English, the marks are used to avoid writing the same thing several times. They are sometimes found in DIY instructions:

Place Section A on a flat surface.
,,   ,,   B at right angles to Section A.

Occasionally, *do*, the abbreviated form of *ditto* is used:

Parallelograms on the same base and between the same parallels are equal in area.
Do   parallelograms on equal bases.

In all but the most informal of styles, the use of ditto marks and 'do' should be avoided.

Ellipsis

Ellipsis (plural ellipses) functions as both a separator and a terminator. The name comes from the Greek verb *elleipein* meaning 'to leave out', 'fall short'. The term is first recorded in written English in 1540 and is represented by a series of full stops [...]. Traditionally, these have been spaced stops but there is a tendency in contemporary writing to leave out the spaces. Ellipsis has three main uses:

1   to indicate the omission of one or more words from a poetic quotation:

But the ... student is bred to the purple, his training in syntax

Is also a training in thought
And even in morals;

(Louis MacNeice, 'Autumn Journal')

When a full line or a stanza has been omitted, a full line of
spaced full stops is sometimes used:

A woman's face, with Nature's own hand painted,

....

A woman's gentle heart ...   (Shakespeare, Sonnet XX)

It is not necessary to use ellipses at the beginnings and ends
of quotations if these are integrated into the commentary:

John might best be described as in Shakespeare's eulogy
for Brutus:
His life was gentle, and the elements
So mixed in him, that Nature might stand up
And say to all the world, 'This was a man!'

(*Julius Caesar*)

2   to indicate that words, sentences or paragraphs have been
omitted from prose:

Several articles or parts of articles are selected so that the
students have a range of information in front of them ... If
extracts covering the whole story are used ... students
can be asked to arrange them in chronological order.

If the word preceding the ellipsis coincides with the end of a
sentence, the terminator is also included, especially where
this is a question or exclamation mark:

How improbable it was that there would be another friend
there beside Gogol! ... Was this adamantine stare after all
only the awful sneer of some threefold traitor, who had
turned for the last time?

(G. K. Chesterton, *The Man Who Was Thursday*)

Conservative scholars apply this rule to the full stop also:

There are many grammatical differences between British
and American English.... The following discussion presents only some of the more important points of
difference.

Some writers prefer to use only three dots in these
circumstances:

There are many grammatical differences between British

and American English ... The following discussion presents only some of the more important points of difference.

3   to leave something to the imagination of a reader. This technique is often used in advertising:

There's nothing like snuggling down into your own bed on a cold winter's night. We've put together the best quality collection of duck and goose pillows and duvets, cotton flannelette sheets and duvet covers, all to make that moment just a little bit more special ...

in summaries and blurbs for love stories:

They clung to each other. Nothing would ever part them again. Nothing ever could ...

and in headlines:

The details of THAT phonecall ...

Emboldening

Emboldening is a device used in printing to emphasize a piece of language by using a heavier type. The term *boldface*, to refer to the heavy type, came into the language towards the end of the nineteenth century. It is used contrastively with light face. Bold face is widely used for headlines, chapter headings, titles and dictionary entries. This method of emphasizing has become popular with the widespread use of personal computers.

Exclamation mark

The exclamation mark is a terminator. It is referred to as an exclamation *mark* in the United Kingdom and as an exclamation *point* in the United States of America. It is represented by [!]. The first recorded use of the term dates back to 1657, when J. Smith described it as: 'A note of Exclamation or Admiration, thus noted!'

Shakespeare uses the phrase 'notes of admiration' in *The Winter's Tale*. The exclamation mark follows the last letter of the exclamation, without an intervening space:

What a cricketer Lara is!

It tends to be used for three main purposes:

- to indicate involuntary utterances:
  Wow! (and its equivalents)
- to suggest strong emotion:
  Send war in our time, O Lord!
  > (W. B. Yeats, 'Under Ben Bulben')
- to emphasize a statement:
  That's your lot!
  She was utterly beautiful!

A bracketed exclamation mark is sometimes used to call attention to something unusual, unexpected or untrue:

> He was charming (!) and witty but his eyes remained cold.

Occasionally, it is repeated:

> We named the horse! We named the race!! We got it right!!!

Such repetition may be typographically effective, but is to be avoided in serious writing. Overuse of the exclamation mark is associated with 'gushing'. It is better to say exactly what we want with words than to hope that punctuation marks will compensate for inadequate expression.

Headlines often include exclamation marks and their use tends to differ between tabloids and broadsheets. In the former, they are often one-word headlines, sometimes with modified orthography as in the *Sun*'s (in)famous headline about the sinking of the *Belgrano* during the Falklands War: 'GOTCHA!'

Broadsheets tend to use them to remind readers of other occasions. Thus, in the *Sunday Times* (5 December 1993), the following headlines occurred:

> Taxed! And we didn't feel a thing
> Gotcha! Shuttle grabs the telescope in space rescue

Both headlines are appropriate summaries of the stories beneath them, but both also remind readers of other headlines, slogans or catch-phrases. The first is patterned on a much-quoted utterance from the Victorian melodrama, *East Lynne*: 'Dead! And ... never called me mother.' The second is, of course, derived from the *Sun*.

Many readers will not be certain of the reference. We find such headlines striking, however, because they remind us, consciously or unconsciously, of something else.

Occasionally, the exclamation mark is used with other punctuation marks, especially in cartoons. *The Times* (24 December 1993) ran an article on President Clinton with a cartoon whose caption was: 'Sex?! At last – A Clinton story we can understand!'

Footnote

A footnote is an explanation, comment or reference that is usually placed below the text at the bottom of a page. (*Endnotes* are similar to footnotes but occur at the end of a chapter or essay.) The term dates back to 1822 and is a feature of scholarly works. Footnotes have been indicated by asterisks (*), daggers (or obelisks) (†) and double daggers (‡). Today, they are most frequently indicated by superscript figures, numbered consecutively throughout the article or chapter. The footnote number is always an Arabic numeral. It follows any punctuation marks and is not itself followed by a full stop:

> 'There's nothing more to say, then,' he replied. 'Tomorrow to fresh fields and pastures new!'[1]

> 1   The poet John Milton wrote 'woods' not 'fields' in *Lycidas*:
>
> > At last he rose, and twitched his mantle blue:
> > Tomorrow to fresh woods, and pastures new.

SEE ALSO: *asterisk, dagger, obelisk*

Full stop

The full stop is the most frequently used terminator in the language. This punctuation mark, represented by [.], was called a *point* by Chaucer, a *full point* by Puttenham and both a *full stop* and a *period* by Shakespeare:

> Where I have seen them shiver and look pale,
> Make periods in the midst of sentences.
>
> > (*A Midsummer Night's Dream*)

Today, full stop is the term most widely used in Britain, whereas period is preferred in the United States. Period derives from Greek *periodos*, meaning a 'circuit'. The term was first used in England in 1530 to refer not to the end mark, but to the entire sentence. (Such shifts in meaning are not uncommon in English. A *brat*, for example, used to refer to the shawl in which a child, usually a poor child, was carried. Later, the term came to designate the child.)

This punctuation mark is used for six main purposes:

1   to indicate the end of a sentence that is not an exclamation or a question:

> So she set to work, and very soon finished off the cake.
>
> (*Alice in Wonderland*)

> Good reading always shows.
>
> (Advertisement for the *Yorkshire Post*)

In English, a sentence is not always easy to define, but it is usually an independent grammatical unit that begins with a capital letter and ends with a full stop. A sentence that does not contain a finite verb is called a minor sentence:

> Over to you.

> Always the best for value.

2   to mark abbreviations that end with a lower-case letter, e.g. *Gk.* for 'Greek' or *Lat.* for 'Latin'. In Britain, there is a growing tendency to avoid full stops in all abbreviations (including these), but especially in those which involve the first and last letter in the word:

> Corporal > Cpl
>
> Doctor > Dr
>
> Mister > Mr

The British also now tend to avoid full stops after initials, so that many people write:

> Dr J Jones

Americans generally prefer:

> Dr. J. Jones.

Some abbreviations, however, never take a full stop in either country. These include the abbreviations for currency, weights and measures:

£5 = $7
2oz
6ft

3   to end footnotes. Footnotes, even when they do not contain
    a finite verb, are conventionally treated like full sentences:
        1 Quoted from 1992 edition.
4   to mark the end of proverbs or well-known expressions,
    even when these are verbless:
        Always a bridesmaid, never a bride.
        A newspaper – not a snoozepaper.
        The same two dogs on the same piece of string.
5   between dollars and cents, pounds and pence:
        $5.95
        £4.21
6   to end a list of examples which is used in a sentence:
        The following words are almost synonymous:
        exhaust
        fatigue
        tire
        weary.

Increasingly, the full stop is also used to indicate decimals:

> Express 0.75 as a fraction.
> If a cake is divided equally among all the children at a party
> and each child gets 0.125 of the cake, how many children
> are at the party?

The full stop should **not** be used:

- after an exclamation mark or question mark that appears in
  quotation marks at the end of a sentence:
      *I do not know the words of 'Where have all the flowers
      gone?'.
- after a title, such as that of an essay or book, unless the title
  ends the sentence:
      Language in the USA. is published by Cambridge.
      You should read *Language in the USA.*
- after footnote numbers:
      Crystal[1] also makes this point.

- at the end of items in a table:

	Singular	Plural
1	mi	wi
2	yu	yu
3	i	dem

- after an abbreviation that has a full stop after it:
     *It happened at 2 a.m..

SEE ALSO: *abbreviations, sentence*

Grave accent

The grave [`] rhymes with *halve* and not *pave*. The word was adopted into the language in the sixteenth century, deriving from Latin *gravis*, meaning 'heavy'. This accent, when placed over a vowel, serves two main purposes:

- it suggests that the vowel differs in quality from its unaccented equivalent. Thus the *à* in *à propos* is pronounced differently from the unstressed 'a' in *a nice day*.
- it indicates that the vowel over which the grave accent occurs is to be pronounced separately. Thus *blessed* has one syllable in:
     He blessed the ancient mariner
  and two syllables in:
     the Blessèd Virgin Mary.

SEE ALSO: *accent marks*

Hash

The hash or hash mark, represented by (#), is one of the newest symbols in the language. The recorded use of 'hash' dates back only to the early years of the twentieth century. In Japan and the United States it is a popular means of indicating 'number':

40 Chikusa-ku
1234 Shady Palms Drive.

In the United States, the symbol occasionally follows a number and represents 'pound' (weight):

2 ten # sacks of flour.

Hyphen

A hyphen is a separator. The word derives from Greek *hyph'hen*, meaning 'under one'. It was first referred to in English in 1620 and is represented by [-]. The hyphen is used for seven main purposes:

1 It can mark compound words:
    daughter-in-law
    good-for-nothing
    man-o'-war.
As well as the compound nouns, illustrated above, compounds include:
    prefix + noun:
       post-war
    prefix + verb:
       re-issue
    adjectives formed from phrases or even sentences:
       Publicity-shy prince urges media chiefs to call off newshounds
       her off-the-shoulder-dress
       that I-couldn't-care-less expression.
These hyphenated adjectives only precede the noun. If the phrases follow a verb they are not hyphenated:
    The prince is publicity shy.
    Her dress was off the shoulder.
co-ordinated compounds:
    four- and six-horse teams
    inter- and intra-national communication
in writing out numbers between 21 and 99:
    twenty-seven

     two hundred and sixty-eight

in writing out fractions that precede nouns:

     a one-third majority

     a one-eighth drop in profits.

2   It can mark a division in a word, usually at the end of a line. The rules for word division are simple.

- Avoid it, if possible.
- Never divide a monosyllabic word.
- Never divide a word so as to cause ambiguity:

     export-er *not* *ex-porter

     re-appear *not* *reap-pear.

- Divide the word according to etymology:

     geo-graphy

     trans-port rather than tran-sport.

- Divide the word after the prefix:

     inter-mediary

     sub-marine

- or before the suffix:

     laugh-able

     mod-ish.

- Divide between two consonants:

     estab-lish

     forget-ting

  except when one of the consonants is silent:

     psalm-ist

     talk-ative

  or when the two consonants combine to form one sound, as with 'th', 'ch' and 'gh':

     fath-om

     mach-ismo

     laugh-able.

- Divide after the first consonant where three co-occur:

     chil-blain

     hun-dreds

     illus-trate.

- Divide before the consonant when there is only one:

     cei-ling

     imme-diate.

3 It can be used to mark the morphemes (segments) in a word:
     de-con-struct-ion
     re-ad-miss-ible.
4 It can be used to indicate spelling:
     The word is g-r-a-m-m-a-r. Marks will be deducted if the
     word is misspelt.
5 It can be used as a humorous or literary device to indicate
   stammering:
     K-K-K-Katy, beautiful Katy,
     You're the only g-g-g-girl that I adore.
6 It can be used to compress information in headlines:
     Dad-to-be PC in soccer pitch tragedy
     Go-ahead for comprehensives.
7 It can be used to signal a common second element in all the
   items in a list:
     The returns are expected to be two-, three- or even
     fourfold.

Occasionally a double hyphen [=] is used when a hyphenated
word occurs at the end of a printed line. It indicates that the word
should be hyphenated irrespective of its position in the line:

     The managing director boasted that he was a self=
     made man.

It is not possible to give definitive rules according to which
compound words should be hyphenated, partly because there is
an element of personal taste involved, and partly because hyphens
tend to be lost as the compound becomes more widely used.
Usually, when a compound is made up of more than two words, it
is hyphenated, as in *ne'er-do-well*, but even this rule is not
absolute, as we can see from:

     albeit (<all + be + it)
     nevertheless (never + the + less)
     whodunnit (<who + done + it).

Compounds involving two items are the most difficult to categor-
ize. It is not logical, for example, that:

     all + ready is now already

whereas:

> all + right remains all right

and:

> all + round becomes all-round (an all-round athlete)

and, yet, this is standard practice. The tendency is for compounds to start off as two separate words:

> book keeper.

As the two words co-occur more frequently, they tend to be hyphenated:

> book-keeper.

If the two words fuse to create a new word whose meaning is different from the meanings of the individual words, the compound is usually written as if it were one word, as in:

> bookworm.

There are also some differences between British and American usage, with Americans, on the whole, using fewer hyphens. It is advisable to check usage in an up-to-date dictionary, but the following points should help:

- Noun compounds involving letters + nouns are usually written with hyphens:
  G-string
  S-bend
  T-bone
  U-turn
  X-ray.
- Noun compounds involving adverbs or prepositions are usually written with hyphens:
  hanger-on
  passer-by
  spin-off
  take-over.

- Noun compounds involving verb forms are usually written with a hyphen:
    do-gooder
    has-been
    put-down
    who-done-it.
- Noun compounds whose meanings are no longer literal are usually written without spaces or hyphens:
    blackguard
    horsepower
    waistcoat
    Whitsun.
- Noun compounds that have been in frequent use for a period of time are often written without spaces and hyphens:
    footprint
    hairpin
    handbag
    raincoat.

Adjective compounds have been a feature of the English language for a thousand years:

anhyrnd (one-horned)
micelheafded (big-headed)
yrremod (wild-tempered).

Adjective compounds can occur in two positions, namely, before a noun:

a self-made man
a two-faced individual

and after linking verbs, such as *be*, *become* and *seem*:

They were both self made.
We must have seemed two faced.

Usually, the compound adjectives that follow verbs are not hyphenated. It is not always easy to generalize about a category that is so large, but the following rules should be of help:

- Adjective compounds of more than two words are hyphenated when they occur before a noun:

  an off-the-cuff remark

  an up-and-coming singer

  that never-to-be-forgotten moment

  his famous come-with-me-to-the-Casbah smile.

- Adjective compounds made up of noun/adjective + past participle are hyphenated when they occur before a noun:

  The book is called *The Purple-eared Monster*.

  big-boned (youth)

  child-centred (learning)

  hand-knitted (garments).

- Adjective compounds made up of noun/adjective + present participle are hyphenated when they occur before a noun:

  hard-working (people)

  long-lasting (relationships)

  finger-lickin' (chicken)

  money-making (schemes).

- Adjective compounds made up of adjective + noun are hyphenated when they occur before a noun:

  big-time (crook)

  high-fibre (diet)

  long-distance (call).

- Adjective compounds made up of *self* + noun or adjective or verb are hyphenated when they occur before a noun:

  self-confessed (chocoholic)

  self-evident (truth)

  self-help (scheme).

- Adjective compounds made up of *well* + an adverb or verb are hyphenated when they precede a noun:

  a well-bred person *but* he is well bred.

  a well-off surgeon *but* she is well off.

  If 'very' precedes the compound adjective, it is not hyphenated:

  a very well-bred person.

- Adjective compounds made up of number + noun or verb

are hyphenated when they occur before a noun:

a three-piece (suite)
three-handed (bridge)
a two-horse (race)
a two-pronged (attack).

Traditionally, an en-rule dash rather than a hyphen was used for page references:

pp. 15–95

for indicating 'up to and including'

1939–45

and for compounded proper nouns used adjectivally:

the Sapir–Whorf hypothesis.

Increasingly, the hyphen is used for these purposes, too.

SEE ALSO: *compounding, dash*

Icons

Icons such as ☎ to represent a telephone as in:

☎ 0171-221-1111

are not, strictly speaking, punctuation marks. We refer to them here because of their increased use as a shorthand device in the written medium. In addition, there is no easy cut-off point between icons and other widely used symbols such as:

∵   because
∴   therefore
„   ditto
=   equals
+   plus
$ dollar
£   pound sterling
number

%   per cent
>   is greater than; becomes
<   is less than; is derived from.

The most widely used icons in Britain are:

   no smoking

parking

restaurant service

washroom facilities

wheelchair facilities.

As many of these icons are available on personal computers, it seems likely that their popularity will increase. Many of the icons and symbols referred to above are doubly useful. They are a simple way of saying a great deal unambiguously, and many of them can be interpreted irrespective of the language we speak.

Italics

The word *italic* was used in English in the fifteenth century to refer to a style of cursive handwriting that slanted to the right. Today, it refers to a typestyle or font as in: *These words are italicized.* Normal print is referred to as roman.

Partly because of the cost of changing typefaces, italics were used sparingly in printing, but it is conventional to use them for the following purposes:

- for emphasis:
    What did he say?
  If the entire sentence is italicized, then the emphasized word is not in italics:
    What did *he* say?*
- for the titles of ballets, books (but not the Bible, books of the Bible or the Koran), films, journals, long poems, major musical compositions, magazines, plays and operas:
    Delia Chiaro's *The Language of Jokes*

Handel's *Messiah*
Milton's *Paradise Lost*
Spielberg's *E.T.*
Woman's Own is sold weekly.

If the title occurs in a sentence that is italicized, the title is in roman letters:

I haven't read Paradise Lost *since I was at school.*

Quotation marks and not italics are used for the titles of articles, chapters, songs and short poems and stories:

Her article, 'Pidgins and Creoles: a millennium report', is worth reading.

Did 'Puppet on a String' win the Eurovision Song Contest?

Who wrote 'The Tell-tale Heart'? Was it Poe?

There is some vacillation between italics and quotation marks for references to radio and television programmes:

'The Bill' is celebrating its tenth anniversary.

(What's on TV?)

The anniversary episode of *The Bill* is a must.

(What's on TV?)

The well-known programmes are most likely to be italicized.

University Challenge is appealing to a new generation of viewers.   *(Sunday Times)*

● for the names of aircraft, railway engines, ships and spacecraft:

Virgin's *Lady in Red* was launched by Princess Diana.

the *Blue Arrow*

HMS *Invincible*

the spaceship *Columbia*.

When apostrophe + s occur with such a name, they are not in italics:

Invincible's last port of call.

● for words and phrases that have been borrowed from other languages but that have not been fully assimilated into English:

aloha (love)

mores (customs)

dulce et decorum est (it is sweet and seemly)

pour épater le bourgeois (to shock the middle class).

It is not easy to give comprehensive rules about which words and phrases should be italicized. In general, they should not be italicized if they are pronounced as English and if most people know what they mean:

ad infinitum

data

ersatz

garage

motif

sputnik

vamoose.

On the other hand, the following items are normally italicized:

a priori

brouhaha

dolce vita

double entendre

glasnost

nemine contradicente

sensu stricto.

The two most likely to be used widely are *dolce vita* and *glasnost*, both of which are, on occasions, written in roman script.

Roman script should normally be used for proper names and for quotations from other languages:

Napoleon Bonaparte

It's as the French say, 'A bon chat, bon rat'.

In course papers, academic articles, dissertations and theses, italics should be used sparingly. In botanical and zoological studies, italics are conventionally used for the names of genera and species, but roman script for higher ranks (phyla, classes, orders).

The phylum Arthropoda includes the invertebrate animals *arachnids* and *crustaceans*.

Publishers have their own house rules regarding the use of italics for quotations. In academic writing, too, there are no fixed rules. It is conventional, however, for prose quotations of up to 100 words to be incorporated into the text, placed within quotation marks and attributed. Longer quotations are usually italicized; they should not be placed within quotation marks; and they should also be indented. For students who do not have a personal computer or typewriter with italics, it is conventional to use underlining instead.

Books, like this one, will often use indentations and italics as a means of highlighting information, including short quotations.

Italics should be used only where they aid comprehension (to distinguish a book from an article, for example) or where the use is conventionalized.

SEE ALSO: *underlining*

Numbers

There are some rules for dealing with numbers written in English. The most important is to use words for numbers between one and ninety-nine in essays or scholarly writings:

> Yeats uses 'the' eight times in the first section of 'The Second Coming'.
> What, other than seventy-seven, rhymes with eleven and has four syllables?

This generalization does not apply to dates:

> 3 February

to mathematics:

> If it takes 7 men 3 days to build a house, how many men will be needed to build 13 houses in 6 days?

to units of measurement:

> 3 metres

to time:

> It is 11:25 precisely.

to ages, especially in the tabloid press:

> 64-year-old, pedalling pensioner

to house and telephone numbers:

> London W2 4AA, Tel. 0171–221–1234

to chapters, pages or footnotes:

> See Chapter 4, pp. 68–84.

In general, use Arabic numbers. Roman numbers, both capitals and lower case (I, II, X, LX, i, ii, x), are still often used, however, in references to acts and scenes:

> Shakespeare refers to the apostrophe in Act IV, scene ii of *Love's Labour's Lost*.

for rulers:

> Pope John XXIII was succeeded by Pope Paul VI.

and for the preliminary pages in a book:

> The book has 621 pages (xx + 601).

It is conventional for scenes and preliminary pages to use lower-case letters, i.e., i, ii, iii, iv, while acts and rulers are given upper-case letters:

> Louis XIV is supposed to have said: 'L'état, c'est moi!'

Obelisk

This character, more frequently called a dagger because of its shape [†], has functioned as a punctuation mark in English since the sixteenth century. Originally it was shaped like a dash (-) or like the sign for division (÷) and was used to highlight a doubtful item in the text. Today, the dagger symbol is occasionally used for marginal footnotes and references.

SEE ALSO: *dagger*

Oblique mark

The punctuation mark represented by [/] is increasingly referred to as an oblique mark, or simply an oblique, although it is also known as a *diagonal, slash, solidus* and *virgule*.

The oblique is currently used for five main purposes:

1   to separate alternatives:
    and/or
    he/she
    Within twelve months of taking up his/her appointment, the professor will be required to live within twenty-five miles of the campus.   (University contract)
2   to indicate the end of poetic lines when verse is written as if it were prose:
    Though leaves are many, the root is one;/Through all the lying days of my youth/I swayed my leaves and flowers in the sun;/Now I may wither into the truth.
                    (W. B. Yeats, 'The Coming of Wisdom with Time')
3   to mark phonemes:
    In English, the /p/ in 'pat' is voiceless whereas the /b/ in 'bat' is voiced.
4   to imply 'per' in abbreviations:
    The water flow is 6ft/sec (six feet per second).
5   occasionally to separate years:
    This demand relates to the 1994/95 tax year.
    and also days, months and years in dates:
    Date of birth: 31/12/89.

SEE ALSO: *bar, diagonal, slash, solidus, virgule*

Paragraph

The word derives from the Greek *paragraphein* (to write beside). A line or symbol was written in a certain position in order to draw attention to that section of text or to show a change of speaker in a drama. The word was first recorded in English in 1525. Paragraphs developed in prose in much the same way as stanzas developed in verse: to indicate a stage in the development of an argument. The symbol [§] or [[ ] is used by editors to indicate that a new paragraph should be introduced.

A paragraph is a visual aid, signalling a step in an argument or discussion. It is usually signalled by indenting the first word five letter spaces or by leaving a double line space between paragraphs, but not both. The first paragraph of a text is not usually indented; nor are the first paragraphs after a heading or subheading. Publishers have their own house styles with regard to paragraphing, but in general the more conservative publishers, in both Britain and the United States of America, continue to indent.

The written representation of direct speech is indented in novels and stories, but not usually in newspapers:

> 'Yes,' said the Zebra, 'but this isn't the High Veldt. Can't you see?'
>
> 'I can now,' said the Leopard. 'But I couldn't all yesterday. How is it done?'
>
> 'Let us up,' said the Zebra, 'and we will show you.'
>
> (Rudyard Kipling, *Just So Stories*)

Traditionally, therefore, each token of direct speech is treated as a separate paragraph, even though some may be very short.

A paragraph should be constructed in such a way that it contains a main theme supported by one or more subordinate but related points. Successive paragraphs should provide a series of steps in an argument, leading towards a conclusion.

There can be no fixed rules as to the length or complexity of a paragraph. Milton's paragraphs were often long, formally constructed pieces of rhetoric. The modern tendency, possibly influenced by journalism, is to prefer short paragraphs. Some novelists, essayists and philosophers still feel that their subject matter requires longer paragraphs in which ideas and opinions are discussed and evaluated.

Parentheses

Parentheses (singular parenthesis) are separators that are used to provide amplifications or explanations. The word came into

English via Latin and was first recorded in 1568. It comes ultimately from Greek *parentithenai* (to put round). Today, the term parentheses is used for both the round brackets ( ) and for the parenthetical insertion itself. Such parenthetical insertions are most frequently found within round brackets and between dashes:

> She was (everyone admitted) a genius.
> She was – everyone admitted – a genius.
> Watch out for manga cartoons – demented full-length adult animation films – and for cyberpunk movies, a sort of Dr Who for grown-ups.   (*Sunday Times*)

SEE ALSO: *brackets, dashes*

Question mark

The question mark is a terminator that is symbolized by [?]. The expression was introduced into English as recently as 1869 to refer to the punctuation mark that concludes an interrogation:

> And what shoulder, and what art,
> Could twist the sinews of thy heart?
> And when thy heart began to beat,
> What dread hand? and what dread feet?
>
> (William Blake, 'The Tiger')

The question mark is used mainly for the following purposes:

● to mark the end of a sentence which is a direct question:
   'When was he born?' I asked.
   I asked, 'When was he born?'
It is not placed after a question in indirect speech:
   I asked when he was he born.
and not:
   *I asked when was he born?
The question mark is put after the precise question that is asked and not, necessarily, at the end of the sentence:
   'When was he born?' I asked.
and not:
   *'When was he born?' I asked?

- to mark truncated questions:
  Pillory, or Fowler howler?   (*Sunday Times* headline)
  Name? (i.e., What is your name?)
  Address?
  Date of birth?
- to indicate uncertainty, especially about dates:
  Jean Froissart (?1337–1410)
- to indicate an intonational question, that is, a question which is identical in form to a statement. In speech, the intonation signals that it is a question; in the written medium, the question mark serves the same purpose:
  You're really going? You won't change your mind?
- to indicate rhetorical questions which are really the equivalent of an emphatic statement:
  Was he handsome? = He was extremely handsome.

Question marks are also used to indicate that a linguistic structure is only marginally acceptable:

?I have been being followed all day.

or to denote a bad move in chess reports:

1   Bxh2 + !;
?2   Nxh2 Qg6 +

Quotation marks

Quotation marks are separators. The term was first recorded in English in 1883. Quotation marks may be single ['] or double ["]. They are also known as inverted commas and, more recently, as quotes. Single quotation marks are preferred in Britain, while double quotation marks are the norm in the United States. Many people in Britain, however, prefer to use double quotation marks and consistency of usage is more important than dogma. In both Britain and the United States, quotation marks are used for five main purposes:

1   to enclose quotations of direct speech:
    'I love you,' he said, 'so dearly.' (mainly British)

"I love you," he said, "so dearly." (US)

and to indicate the speech of different individuals in a conversation:

'Are you very angry with me?'

'No. Not at all. Only – only I must be left to myself for a while. Don't move. I'm going to bed.'

(W. Somerset Maugham, 'The Force of Circumstance')

If the direct quotation runs to several paragraphs, it is conventional to place opening quotation marks at the beginning of each paragraph, but closing quotation marks once only, at the end of the quotation:

And he said, 'A certain man had two sons. And the younger one said to his father: "Father, give me the portion of goods that falleth to me." And he divided unto them his living. And not many days after the younger son gathered all together, and took his journey into a far country, and there wasted his substance with riotous living.

'And when he had spent all, there arose a mighty famine in that land, and he began to be in want.'

(St Luke, Chapter 15)

2 to enclose quotations of up to about a hundred words from printed material:

Jespersen claimed that similar results sprang from similar causes; in this case, the 'imperfect mastery of a language which in its initial stage, in the child with its first language and in the grown-up with a second language learnt by imperfect methods, leads to a superficial knowledge of the most indispensable words, with total disregard of grammar'.

Paraphrases are not enclosed within quotation marks. Unacknowledged paraphrases may, however, be regarded as plagiarism.

3 for the titles of short stories, short poems, chapters in books, lectures, radio and television programmes, songs and short musical works:

Edgar Allan Poe's greatest short story is probably 'The Pit and the Pendulum'. (British)

Edgar Allan Poe's greatest short story is probably "The Pit and the Pendulum." (US)

4   to highlight quoted words or phrases:

He said he'd be 'early', but I didn't believe him! (British)
He said he'd be "early," and I believed him! (US)

The comma is enclosed within the quotation marks in the United States, but other quotation marks fall outside them:

He said he'd be 'early'; I didn't believe him! (British)
He said he'd be "early"; I didn't believe him! (US)

5   to highlight dialect or slang words if they are out of keeping with a particular style:

It is not easy to find a standard equivalent for 'munchee-man'. (British)
It is not easy to find a standard equivalent for "munchee-man". (US)

In Britain, double quotation marks are used for a quotation within a quotation. The reverse is true in the United States of America:

'What do you mean by "soon"?' I asked. (British)
"What do you mean by 'soon'?" I asked. (US)

A number of generalizations can be made that apply to both Britain and the United States of America.

- Quotation marks are not used when a passage is set in a different type, for example, in italics.
- Quotation marks are not used for *yes* or *no* unless they are being treated as direct speech:

    He didn't say yes to any of our suggestions.

- Alteration to a quotation must be clearly indicated, using the appropriate punctuation marks. Additions are marked by square brackets, omissions by ellipsis:

    Cracking a sea louse, [he] make[s] thunder split.

    (Derek Walcott, 'The Castaway')

    That sail in cloudless light
    which tires of islands ...   (Derek Walcott, 'Sea Grapes')

- All punctuation marks belonging to the passage are placed inside the quotation marks; all those belonging to the person quoting are placed outside:

I love the phrase 'paradoxical ratiocination'!

She wrote, 'I love the phrase "paradoxical ratiocination"!'

When a sentence ends with a quotation that ends with a full stop, a question mark, an exclamation mark or ellipsis, it is not necessary to add another full stop:

He said, 'Here's a penny, son.'

He asked, 'Have you got a penny, Mister?'

He said, 'What! Just a penny!'

He started, 'Here's a penny, son ...'

- Prose quotations of up to ten typed lines or about a hundred words are usually given within quotation marks and incorporated into the text. Longer quotations are not given within quotation marks. They are separated from the text and indented on the left-hand side. A colon is normally used to introduce a longer quotation. (Some writers prefer to indent and separate from their text all quotations of more than ten words. Again, consistency is more important than dogma.)

SEE ALSO: *italics* and Section 3

Round brackets

Round brackets ( ) are separators and are the most widely used brackets today. They are also called *parentheses* (singular *parenthesis*) because they enclose parenthetic, that is, explanatory or supplementary material. Round brackets are used for eight main purposes:

1   to include supplementary information:

But there was no information, and so we continued
And arrived at evening, not a moment too soon
Finding the place; it was (you may say) satisfactory.

(T. S. Eliot, 'Journey of the Magi')

The old ship (surplus now to requirements) was sold for scrap.

> Applications (10 copies, which should be typed) together with the names and addresses of three referees should be sent to the Personnel Office.

If the supplementary information is a complete sentence, it takes a capital letter and a terminator inside the brackets:

> The announcement of the cabinet reshuffle (Details had already been well trailed.) was something of an anticlimax.

> We started out early (You know us!) and got there an hour too soon.

Many stylists dislike the use of complete sentences within brackets, suggesting that this technique should be avoided. Our examples above, from a Sunday broadsheet and a personal letter, show that writers do not always follow the advice of purists.

2   to indicate options:

> Please indicate the module(s) you would like to take in the first semester. If you list more than one, please list them in order of preference.

> The winner(s) will receive a cheque for £25,000 and guaranteed book sales.

3   to enclose abbreviations for full forms, especially when these are cumbersome:

> A Joint Negotiating Committee (JNC) for Academic and Related Staff has been established with the University Authorities Panel (UAP) representing the Universities [*sic*] Side and the Association of University Teachers (AUT) representing employees.

4   to enclose the full form for abbreviations or acronyms that may not be widely known:

> Most major computer manufacturers have an involvement in RISC (Reduced Instruction Set Computer). Acorn's ARM (Acorn Risc Machine) chip has proved successful, at the centre of Acorn's Archimedes computer and as a component in add-ons. (*What Micro?* Dictionary)

5   to enclose numbers or letters in a series:

> We have introduced these modifications (1) to offer schools and candidates the opportunity to explore the

potential of the language in ways that are ordered, sensitive, stimulating and interesting; (2) to integrate the teaching of language and literature; (3) to encourage candidates to study and understand ...

6   to confirm a written number or day:

If payment has not been made within twenty-eight (28) days, legal action will ensue.

Full payment must be made within sixty (60) days.

I shall arrive next Monday (August 25) at 17:30.

Looking forward to seeing you tomorrow (Tuesday).

7   to provide a person's dates or age:

Among the most talented of these dramatists was Christopher Marlowe (1564–93).

The first person to helicopter round the world was Texan Ross Perot (23).

8   to attribute a reference:

The mind can also be an erogenous zone.

(Raquel Welch)

Old age isn't so bad when you consider the alternative.

(Ronald Reagan)

SEE ALSO: *brackets, parentheses*

Semicolon

The semicolon is a separator represented by [;]. It derives from Latin *semi*, 'half' + Greek *kolon*, 'part of a verse', and its recorded use in English dates back to 1644. A semicolon is intermediate in weight between a comma and a full stop, and it is unique among punctuation marks in that its use is never obligatory. The semicolon has three main purposes in English:

1   to link clauses that are the equivalent of independent sentences but are closely related in meaning:

Some are born great; some achieve greatness; and some have greatness thrust upon 'em.   (*Twelfth Night*)

Let us make this a country safe to work in; let us make this a country safe to walk in; let us make this a country safe to grow up in ...   (Margaret Thatcher)

Often, as above, the structures linked by semicolons are rhetorically balanced.

2   to avoid overusing conjunctions in balanced utterances, made up of dyads (two elements):

I used to be conceited, but I got over it; now I'm perfect.

and triads (three elements):

We arrived; we had dinner; we left.

3   to avoid overusing conjunctions in lists, especially where the list may contain groupings of several words:

We sell books, journals and magazines; we sell pens, pencils and papers; we sell everything that the student needs.

The well-used semicolon gives balance and a sense of order to a piece of writing. Perhaps that explains its popularity in sermons, political speeches and rhyming couplets:

God made the first Marriage, and man made the first Divorce; God married the Body and Soul in the Creation, and man divorced the Body and Soul by death through sin, in his fall.   (John Donne, 'Corruption and Redemption')

You turn if you want to; the lady's not for turning.
(Margaret Thatcher, 1980 Conservative Conference)

But at my back I always hear
Time's wingèd chariot hurrying near;
And yonder all before us lie
Deserts of vast eternity.
(Andrew Marvell, 'To His Coy Mistress')

Sentence

The simplest definition of a sentence is that it begins with a capital letter and ends with a full stop:

Okay.
By Bus, By Train, Buy Metro.
Here you are.

If you look carefully, you will see something that looks a little like a boat.

Scholars have spent a great deal of time trying to provide an accurate but comprehensive definition of a sentence, but each definition provided can be challenged. The current view is that a sentence is a grammatically independent unit which can express a statement, a command, a wish, an exclamation or a question. Sentences occur in the written medium and correspond loosely to utterances in speech. An utterance is produced by a specific individual at a specific time and in specific circumstances. It can be affected by such factors as tiredness, boredom, excitement or anger. A sentence, on the other hand, is a feature of the written language and so is not, usually, adversely affected by mood or circumstances.

Sentences can be subdivided in various ways. A *major* sentence contains at least one finite verb. (A finite verb is one that agrees with its subject, e.g. I am, he is.):

That's all, folks.
I heard every word that you said.

A *minor* sentence looks like a sentence in that it begins with a capital letter and ends with a terminator, but it does not contain a finite verb. Minor sentences are widely used in advertising:

Networking? Novell, of course.
Never knowingly undercut.
Going for a song.

Minor sentences are sometimes called elliptical sentences because we can usually supply a word or group of words to convert them into major sentences:

Are you involved in networking? Then you should choose Novell software.
We are never knowingly undercut.
These records are going for a song (i.e. they are very cheap).

Sentences can be statements, either positive or negative:

Students opting for this course will need a good working knowledge of the structure of English.

> This option will not be available during the 1995–96 academic year.

Statements end with a full stop.

Sentences may be imperatives, that is they may give orders:

> Sign here, please.
> Don't forget the fruit gums, Mum.

These, too, end with full stops. Sentences may be in the form of questions and end with a question mark:

> Can you direct me to the Cricket Ground?
> Don't you like it?

or they may be exclamations and end with an exclamation mark:

> I hate you!
> You must be mad!

Writers sometimes use what linguists call *fused sentences*, that is, they use commas where the use of 'and', full stops or semicolons would be more appropriate:

> This elegant house benefits from partial double glazing, it has fully lawned gardens to the front and rear.
>
> (House advertisement, 1994)

These sentences should not be separated by a comma. They would be better as:

> This elegant house benefits from partial double glazing and it has fully lawned gardens to the front and rear.

or as:

> This elegant house benefits from partial double glazing; it has fully lawned gardens to the front and rear.

> SEE ALSO: *capitalization, full stop*

Slash

A slash is a separator. The word probably comes from Old French *esclachier*, meaning 'to break'. It is also known as a *diagonal*, an *oblique mark,* a *solidus* and, in the United States of America, as a *virgule.*

SEE ALSO: *bar, diagonal, oblique mark, solidus, virgule*

Solidus

The solidus is a separator. The word comes from Latin *solidus,* meaning 'solid'. It was used in printing for [/], a sloping line used to separate shillings and pence, as in 17/6, meaning 'seventeen shillings and sixpence'. (The *s* in LSD is from *solidus,* referring to 'shilling'; *d* is from *denarius* and denoted 'pence'.)

SEE ALSO: *bar, diagonal, oblique mark, slash, virgule*

Square brackets

Square brackets [ ] are separators. They are used for six main purposes:

1   to mark parentheses within parentheses:
George Chapman (?1559–?1634 [neither date is certain]) is chiefly known for his translation of Homer, commemorated in Keats's sonnet 'Much have I travelled in the realms of gold'.
2   to clarify meaning:
Kenneth Clarke and his opposite number crossed swords in the Commons. He [Kenneth Clarke] gave a rumbustious performance on Tuesday.
3   to provide stage directions in plays:
BOY: Joee!
JO: Coming.
[They move towards each other as if dancing to the music. The music goes, the lights change.]
(Shelagh Delaney, *A Taste of Honey*)
4   to indicate that a mistake has occurred, [*sic*] is written after the mistake as in:
... with the University Authorities Panel (UAP) representing the Universities [*sic*] Side ...

where Universities' Side would be correct. The convention [*sic*] from Latin *sic* meaning 'so, thus' is also used to indicate that the text provided is accurately reproduced. Thus, an editor of Shakespeare's *Twelfth Night* might write:

O' the twelfe [*sic*] day of December

to indicate that the form 'twelfe', not 'twelfth', appears in the First Folio, 1623.

5   to mark editorial intrusions into quotations, i.e. when an editor feels that an explanation or clarification is essential:

Our mother tongue is our means of dealing with reality ... if [it] embodies prejudice, then we are all disadvantaged.

6   to enclose and signal phonetic script:

Many speakers pronounce 'cat' [kʰæt].

Brackets are often used in grammatical analyses in Britain. Round brackets mark off words and phrases; square brackets mark off clauses and sentences. Sometimes, the bracketing can be complex, not to say off-putting. A sentence such as:

What you said could have been overheard by the people who were travelling on the bus hired for the football match.

would be represented by:

[[(What) (you) (said)] (could have been overheard) (by (the people)) [(who) (were travelling) (on (the bus [hired for the football match]))]).]

We have not included the class or function labels for this analysis.

SEE ALSO: *brackets*

Tags

Tags are not punctuation marks but users of English are often uncertain which punctuation marks co-occur with them. Tags are always preceded by a comma. The commonest tags are question tags involving an auxiliary verb plus a pronoun:

He's coming, isn't he?

> You're not going, are you?
> She scored, didn't she?

If the sentence is positive, the question tag is negative; if the sentence is negative, the tag is positive. Question tags are, of course, followed by question marks.

Occasionally, the tag is used for the purpose of telling, rather than asking:

> You missed it, didn't you!

When the intention is clearly to indicate *and I told you so*, an exclamation mark, rather than a question mark is used.

Tilde

The tilde [˜] is not widely used in English but it occurs in Spanish words that have been adopted into the language or are well known outside Spain. The word came into English in the nineteenth century and derives ultimately from Latin *titulus* (title). The tilde is used over an 'n' to indicate that the 'n' is pronounced like 'ny'.

SEE ALSO: *accent marks, brackets*

Umlaut

The umlaut is represented by [¨] as in German *Köln* and *über*. The word comes from German *um* 'around' and *Laut* 'sound' and was first recorded in English in 1844. It indicates a change in vowel sound. The umlaut mark is identical to dieresis. It is possible to replace the umlaut with 'e', however, as in *Koeln* and *ueber*. The dieresis is often dropped, but never replaced by 'e'.

SEE ALSO: *accent marks, dieresis*

Underlining

Underlining is a convention used in typing and printing. It is sometimes used where italics are not available. The convention is that all words, phrases or titles which would normally be italicized may be underlined. Tabloid newspapers, which have italics available, often use underlining as an additional form of emphasis, particularly for sub-headings:

<u>Puzzled</u>   (*Daily Express*)

SEE ALSO: *italics*

Virgule

The term virgule was once widely used to indicate a mark, approximately the equivalent of today's comma. The word comes from Latin *virgula* (a small rod or twig). The symbol [/] was used in manuscripts and early printing but has been replaced by [,]. The word virgule is still used in the United States as a scholarly alternative to slash.

SEE ALSO: *comma, slash*

Section 3

Punctuation in Use

UK and US usage

The overlap between the English language in Britain and in the United States of America is large and growing, but the differences are significant. Generalizing, one can say that Americans tend to be slightly more conservative in their use of punctuation, often using full stops and commas where they would be omitted by most British writers.

Colon

Many Americans use a colon after terms of address in letters:

> Dear Madam:
> Dear Ms. Brown:
> Dear Myra Brown:

Comma

Americans tend to use more commas than the British. They tend to put them:

- after abbreviations such as e.g. and i.e. when these occur in a sentence:

  > A certain amount of local currency – e.g., francs, marks, and pounds – can also be recommended.

- before the 'and' in lists:

  > Sports available include baseball, basketball, and volleyball.

- between clauses in compound and complex sentences:

We knew nothing about her, and we cared even less.
The man sat down, because he was tired.

● in numbers containing thousands, millions, billions or trillions:

7,642
9,765,723
1,000,000,000
1,000,000,000,000.

The British are now less likely to use commas after thousands:

The holiday of a lifetime for under £1000!

This is, possibly, to reduce problems with other members of the European Community. The French, for example, use a full stop to mark off thousands and millions:

FF1.123.679

Increasingly, too, in Britain, 'K', occasionally 'k', is used for 'thousand', especially in advertisements:

Salary £48K + car + fringe benefits.

Full stop/period

Americans tend to use full stops, which they call periods, after initials:

T. S. Jones
R. Alan Hall

after abbreviated titles:

Dr. Mary S. Evans
R. Alan Hall, Jr.
Messrs. John and Michael Penrose

after abbreviations:

e.g.
etc.
i.e.

in lists:

A.   Requirements:
1.   Ability to cook
2.   Ability to drive

The decimal point used to be in the middle:

·75

This centrally placed dot is now almost always replaced by a full stop in both Britain and the United States of America.

In all of the instances cited above, we find overlap between British and American usage. Many people in Britain, for example, also use full stops after initials, as in:

T. S. Jones

and after scholarly abbreviations such as i.e.

Quotation marks

Americans prefer double quotation marks to indicate direct speech:

"Mine is a long and sad tale!" said the Mouse, turning to Alice, and sighing.
"It's a long tail, certainly," said Alice, "but why do you call it sad?"

For quotations within quotations, single marks are used:

"I never heard of 'Uglification'," Alice ventured to say. "What is it?"

The comma is usually placed within the outer quotation marks in the United States:

"I never heard of 'Uglification'."

just as it is in Britain.

UK and European usage

This book is intended to describe English punctuation, so it would be out of place to provide detailed comparisons between English usage and that of all other languages of the European Community. It may be of value, however, to provide a few comments:

Dutch

- Lower-case letters are used for the days of the week:
  woensdag 20 juli 1994
  and for months of the year:
  5 mei 1995
- Abbreviations tend to be followed by full stops:
  Dr.
- The equivalent of 'I', *ik*, takes a lower-case letter:
  En ik ben niet meer waardig uw zoon genaamd te worden.
  (And I am no longer worthy to be called your son.)
- It is usual to use a lower-case letter after a brief exclamation:
  Vader! ik heb gezondigd tegen den hemel ... (Father! I have sinned against Heaven ...)
  Kind! gij zijt altijd bij mij, en al het mijne is uwe. (Child! You are always with me, and all that I have is yours.)

French

- The words *madame*, *mademoiselle*, *monsieur* and their plurals are written in full and with no capitalization when they are not followed by a proper noun:
  Où est madame?
  The first letter of the title is capitalized before a proper noun and the title is usually abbreviated:
  M. Hulot et Mme Vernier.
- Accents are often omitted when words are capitalized:
  UNIVERSITE DE YAOUNDE (Université de Yaoundé)
  VOITURE A VENDRE (Voiture à vendre).
- Surnames beginning with *la* usually capitalize the 'l':
  La Fontaine
  M. Jean La Fontaine.
  Names involving *de* or *de la* have a lower-case 'd':

de Vigny.

M. Jean de Vigny.

- Lower-case letters are used for the names of languages:

  L'espagnol se chante; l'allemand se crache; l'anglais se vomit; le français se parle (one sings Spanish; one spits German; one vomits English; one speaks French),

  for adjectives derived from proper nouns:

  les pays européens

  and for days of the week and months of the year:

  lundi, le 31 mars.

- Guillemets (« »), rather than inverted commas, are used to indicate speech:

  Il m'a dit: «Salut, vieux», et il a appelé Marie «mademoiselle».   (Camus, *L'Étranger*)

  A guillemet (‹) is used to open each paragraph belonging to a particular speech. In this way, it parallels the use of quotation marks.

German

- German abbreviations are usually followed by a full stop:

  Dr.

- All German nouns and words used as nouns are given an initial capital letter:

  Musik, Güte.

- A subordinate clause is separated from a main clause by a comma.

- Imperative sentences usually end with an exclamation mark.

- The first word of a letter, after the salutation, does not begin with a capital letter unless the capital is required for some other reason.

- Two commas are used at the beginning of a quotation and two reversed commas at the end. Quotations within quotations open with one comma and close with one reversed comma. Occasionally, reversed guillemets (» ‹) are used to enclose quotations.

Greek

Greek has a different orthography and uses seventeen consonants and seven vowels.

- Sentences do not usually begin with a capital letter.
- In modern Greek, double quotation marks, " ", are preferred.
- The comma (,), exclamation mark (!) and full stop (.) are used in essentially the same way as in English.
- The symbol (?) is not normally used as a question mark. The Greek equivalent is a semicolon (;).
- The symbol (:) is not normally used. The equivalent of the colon in Greek is (·).

Irish

Irish Gaelic is now written with the normal roman alphabet. A *fada* or length mark, is used over some vowels:

> Seán agus mé

and 'h' after a consonant means that the pronunciation of the consonant is modified:

> *bh* is realized as 'v' in *bhí*.

Irish punctuation resembles American in preferring double quotation marks to indicate direct speech and in using more full stops after abbreviations than is usual in English practice:

> The Taoiseach, Mr. Reynolds, then set out his "agenda" for the year.

Italian

- The rules for spacing with apostrophes differ from English usage. In general, there is a space before the apostrophe when the apostrophe replaces a vowel at the beginning of a word:

  > su 'l

  When an apostrophe follows a vowel, there is a space before the next letter:

i' fui

When an apostrophe follows a consonant, there is no space before the next letter:

dall'aver.

- The days of the week, months of the year and the names of languages take lower-case letters.

Spanish

- Spanish uses opening and closing marks to indicate questions and exclamations as well as direct speech. The opening mark is the upside-down version of the closing one:

¿Donde?

¡Increible!

- The days of the week, months of the year and the names of languages take lower-case letters.

Punctuating letters

The punctuation used in writing letters has changed quite considerably over the last twenty-five years. The style now in use is simpler and more straightforward. We shall deal with the subject in terms of two subsections: addressing envelopes; and the opening and the conclusion of letters.

Basically, there are two main styles of letter-writing: blocked and indented. In blocked letters, everything begins at the left-hand margin and there is a double line space between paragraphs. In indented letters, there is no space between the paragraphs, which are indented. The two styles should not be used together.

Addressing envelopes

In the past, the address on the envelope was written or typed as follows:

Mr. J. Brown,
   "Everglades",
      15 West Layton,
         Yorkshire.

The person's name was started approximately 5 centimetres (2 inches) from the top of the envelope and about 5 centimetres from the left-hand edge; full stops were used after all abbreviations and after the last word; each line was indented five spaces and all lines, except the last, ended with a comma. This style is not wrong but it is regarded as dated.

Today, in Britain, indentation and punctuation marks are avoided. All letters, both formal and informal, are set out as follows:

> Mr J Brown
> Everglades
> 15 West Layton
> Yorkshire
> BD19 6BA

The use of Esq. for Esquire as in:

> J. Brown, Esq.,

has virtually disappeared, as has the tradition of addressing a letter to:

> Mrs. John Brown.

American usage is similar to contemporary British norms, except that abbreviations take full stops:

> Mrs. M. Brown, M.A.
> 1216 Palm Beach
> Long Island
> Texas
> TX 12345
> U.S.A.

The exception to this rule is the zip code in which the abbreviations for states are given in capitals, without full stops:

> FL   Florida
> ID   Idaho

Americans prefer U.S.A. to USA or US.

In both countries, there is vacillation about the use of Mrs, Miss and Ms. The rule here is simple. Use the woman's preferred title if you know it. If you do not know it, it is preferable to avoid a title altogether:

Mary Brown, MD   Mary Brown, M.D.

Indeed, there is a growing tendency to follow this rule also for men:

John Brown, MD   John Brown, M.D.

The opening and the conclusion of letters

As with addresses, letter openings and conclusions differ depending on the degree of intimacy or formality required. A friendly letter may open:

> 16 Belle Vue Road
> Leeds LS6 2PP
> Yorkshire
> 7 January 1999

Dear Camilla,
  Thank you for ...

or, depending on the relationship, the salutation may be 'My dear Camilla' or 'Dearest Camilla' or any greeting felt to be appropriate by both correspondents. Increasingly, the comma is being omitted after the name in Britain; in the United States of America, a colon is sometimes used:

Dear Camilla:

A more formal letter may begin with 'Dear Mr Smith'; the most formal may begin with 'Dear Sir' or 'Dear Madam'. In the United States and, increasingly, in Britain, the salutation 'Dear Michael Jones' is used.

In the past, the ending and signature were often on the right-hand side of the paper. Now, partly because of the new technology and partly because of a change in taste, the ending is, like the date, increasingly found on the left-hand side. Occasionally, too, the addressee's name and address occur towards the bottom of the page. This is not common but it is preferred by some companies when they use window envelopes.

The conclusion must be in harmony with the opening. A friendly letter to a relative or close friend may end with:

> *Love,*
> > *Camilla*

or 'With love', 'Lots of love' or similar on a line of its own and with the signature one line below and slightly indented. A letter to a good acquaintance may conclude:

> *Best wishes,*
> > *George*

or with similar salutations, including 'All the best', 'Very best wishes', 'Kindest regards'. In Britain, a less formal letter may end with:

> *Cheers*
> > *Mike*

or:

> *Yours*
> > *Alix*

A letter to a named person which begins with 'Dear Mr Brown' will end with:

> *Yours sincerely,*
> *Camilla Khaleel*

A more formal letter still, beginning 'Dear Sir', 'Dear Madam' or 'Dear Sir or Madam' or 'Dear Sir/Madam', will conclude with:

> *Yours faithfully,*
> *Michael Mann*

In formal, typed letters, it is customary to type the writer's name under the signature:

Yours faithfully,
>   *Michael Mann*
Michael Mann

Often, too, the writer's position is provided:

Yours faithfully,
>   *Michael Mann*
Michael Mann
Senior Marketing Manager

Punctuating direct and indirect speech

Written language is often subdivided into such categories as direct speech, narrative and indirect/reported speech.

Direct speech

Direct speech is meant to reproduce the exact words used by a speaker; the narrative is an account of a story or a series of events; and any speech that is not recorded in a speaker's own words is described as 'indirect' or 'reported'.

A number of conventions have developed to mark out direct speech. In drama, direct speech is indicated by placing the speaker's name, usually in capital letters, at the beginning of the utterance and indenting:

> GEOF: Jo, I don't mind that you're having somebody else's baby. What you've done, you've done. What I've done, I've done.
>
> JO: I like you, Geof, but I don't want to marry you.
>
> (Shelagh Delaney, *A Taste of Honey*)

Quotation marks are not used in the layout for plays, unless there is a quotation within a speech.

> His life was gentle, and the elements
> So mixed in him that Nature might stand up
> And say to all the world, 'This was a man!'
>
> (*Julius Caesar*)

The conventions used in other forms of literature involve the use of quotation marks (also called 'inverted commas') to mark out the exact words of a speaker:

> 'Why don't you tell him to find somewhere else to live?' I said and she laughed.　　　　(Jean Rhys, *Wide Sargasso Sea*)

Attributions of direct speech are treated as part of the sentences in which they occur, and the following rules apply (for ease of reference, the following quotations are taken from Jean Rhys's *Wide Sargasso Sea*):

- Quotation marks are used to indicate the limits of the direct speech. Single quotation marks are preferred in Britain, double quotation marks in the United States.
- When the direct speech is a question or an exclamation, the question or exclamation mark is placed within the quotation marks:

  'What did she say?' I asked.

  'Heavens above!' she cried.
- When the direct speech is a statement, a comma is placed within the quotation marks and the full stop follows the attribution.

  'He wouldn't go. He'd probably try to force us out. I've learned to let sleeping curs lie,' she said.

  Quotation marks are used again for any speech that follows the attribution and the new sentence begins with a capital letter:

  'A child passed,' I said. 'She seemed very frightened when she saw me. Is there something wrong about the place?'
- When the attribution comes in the middle of the sentence, the attribution is followed by a comma and the direct speech after it continues with a lower-case letter:

  'Oh I agree,' the other one said, 'but Annette is such a pretty woman. And what a dancer. Reminds me of that song "light as cotton blossom on the something breeze" or is it air? I forget.'
- Thought is conventionally treated like speech:

  'Would Christophine go if I told her to?' I thought.

Many modern writers create a style sometimes called 'stream of consciousness'. This style attempts to represent the unmonitored flow of thoughts and sensations in a character's mind. Since it does not clearly differentiate thought and speech, quotation marks and verbs of attribution are often omitted:

> Stephen bent forward and peered at the mirror held out to him, cleft by a crooked crack, hair on end. As he and others see me. Who chose this face for me? This dogsbody to rid of vermin. It asks me too. (James Joyce, *Ulysses*)

Indirect speech

Indirect speech, also called reported speech, is a conventional representation of an utterance:

> He said that he was tired.

Direct speech can often be transformed into indirect speech by:

- using a noun or pronoun plus an introductory verb of attribution. The commonest attributive verb is *said*, but different shades of meaning can be indicated by using other verbs such as *begin, cry, imply, insist, muse. wonder*.
- often using *that* after the verb of attribution
- changing the first-person pronoun (*I*) into the third-person pronoun (*he/she*)
- putting the verb back one degree into the past. Thus:
  'I am tired' *becomes* He said that he was tired.
  and:
  'I haven't seen her' *becomes* He said that he hadn't seen her.
- changing verbs such as *bring* and *come* to *take* and *go*:
  'I'll bring it when I come here tomorrow' *becomes* She said that she would take it when she went there the following day.
- changing words such as *here, now, tomorrow* to their remote equivalents *there, then* and *the following day*.
- Quotation marks are not used for indirect speech.
- Exclamation and question marks are replaced by an attributive verb that indicates surprise or questioning:

'I've won!' *becomes* He exclaimed that he had won.
'Who are you?' *becomes* He asked who she was.

It is not always easy, however, to transform direct into indirect speech, as we can see if we take a short extract from 'Little Red Riding Hood':

'Oh Grandma, what big eyes you've got!'
'All the better to see you with, my child.'

This dialogue might become:

Little Red Riding Hood exclaimed that her grandmother had got very big eyes. Her grandmother replied that these helped her to see her grandchild more clearly.

It is obvious from studying even this short sample that the meaning is often changed, sometimes quite fundamentally, when direct speech is transformed. In effect, both speech and its representation in the written medium are much more flexible and subtle than the simple dichotomy 'direct/indirect speech' suggests.

Punctuating a bibliography

Increasingly, students are fulfilling part of their course work by means of essays and projects that may require a bibliography. A bibliography should include a list of the articles and books that have been consulted in the preparation of the essay or project. It may be divided into two sections: Primary Texts and Secondary Texts.

Primary texts consist of the actual source books used as texts; secondary texts consist of any commentaries or criticisms used. For example, if A-level candidates were writing an essay on *Hamlet*, their bibliography might be as follows:

BIBLIOGRAPHY

Primary Texts

Edwards, P. ed. (1985) *The New Cambridge Edition of* Hamlet, Cambridge University Press, Cambridge.

Lott, B. ed. (1986) *The New Swan Edition of* Hamlet, Longman, London.

Secondary Texts

Bailey, J. (1981) *Shakespeare and Tragedy*, Routledge, London.
Charney, M. (1988) *Hamlet's Fictions*, Routledge, London.

There are two main forms of bibliographical reference:

- the author–date system, also called the Harvard system:
  Rhys, Jean (1966) *Wide Sargasso Sea*, André Deutsch, London.
- the author–title system:
  Rhys, Jean *Wide Sargasso Sea*, André Deutsch, London, 1966.

The first form is often more economical in that references are short and succinct and can be made within the body of the text:

'You like you catch fever,' he said. (Rhys, 1966: 88).

The same reference, using the author–title system, would require a footnote. The systems are equally valid. What is important here, as in all aspects of punctuation, is consistency. The following points may prove useful:

- Bibliographies should be arranged alphabetically.
- Each entry should always begin with a capital letter and end with a full stop.
  Rhys, Jean (1928) *Postures*, Chatto & Windus, London.
- Titles of books or journals should be underlined or in italics.
  Rhys, Jean (1928) *Postures*, Chatto & Windus, London.
  Guess, D. (1969) 'A Functional Analysis of Receptive Language and Productive Speech', *Journal of Applied Behaviour Analysis*, 2, pp. 55–64. (Note that the comma comes after the closing quotation mark, i.e. after '. . . Speech'.)
- Titles of articles, essays, stories and short poems should be given in single quotation marks, as above.

- An edited compilation should be given as:

    McArthur, T., ed. (1992) *The Oxford Companion to the English Language*, Oxford University Press, Oxford.

- The surname of the second author of a book by more than one author should be given after the name or initials:

    O'Donnell, W. R. and Loreto Todd (1991) *Variety in Contemporary English*, 2nd edn, Routledge, London.

- Names of newspapers are normally quoted in italics:

    The Times, 1 Jan. 2000.

Punctuation advice

There is no simple maxim that we can use to help us remember when and how punctuation marks should be used in contemporary English. Indeed, it is probably not a good idea to try to memorize rules. It is, however, important to understand why the rules exist and why our choice of punctuation marks is not haphazard.

Correct usage

The following generalizations may help:

- Do not overuse punctuation marks. Use only as many as you need for clarity.
- Do not overuse dashes and exclamation marks, in particular. They are often seen as being stylistically imprecise.
- Remember that there are two main kinds of punctuation markers:

    those that terminate an utterance

    those that separate one part of an utterance from the rest.

    We have called the first type *terminators* and the second type *separators*.

- The terminators in English are:

    full stops (periods)

    exclamation marks

    question marks

    ellipses.

All of these are used to mark the end of an utterance, which may vary in length from one word (or even one sound) to a complex sentence:

No.

Oh!

Really?

Yes ...

It needs qualifications for *t* and *d*, which in Irish, when 'broad', sound not like English *t*, *d*, but more like French *t* in *très*, *d* in *dresser*, the tongue being spread just behind the upper teeth; when 'slender', they are close to the English sounds.   (*Teach Yourself Irish*, 1961: 5)

With the exception of ellipses, which can co-occur with a full stop, the terminators are mutually exclusive, that is, we do not normally have full stops, exclamation marks or question marks occurring together at the end of an utterance. As we have seen from some of the quoted examples, however, some individuals may combine terminators for emphasis or impact. We have found the tendency most in evidence in tabloid headlines.

• The separators are:

apostrophes

brackets

colons

commas

dashes

hyphens

obliques

quotation marks

semicolons.

These separators fall into three categories:

those that can occur only singly:

apostrophes

colons

ellipses

hyphens

semicolons

those that can occur either singly or in pairs:

commas

    dashes

    obliques

and those that can occur only in pairs:

    brackets

    quotation marks.

● The most important generalization is that a writer should use punctuation sparingly and consistently.

Common errors

Correct usage is described in Section 2. Below, we provide a number of points on what a writer should **not** do.

● Do **not** use more than one concluding punctuation mark at the end of a sentence:

    The firm is called Mulberry and Co.

and *not*:

    *The firm is called Mulberry and Co..

Use:

    'What did you say?' I asked.

and *not*:

    *'What did you say?' I asked?

Use:

    You didn't!

and *not*:

    *You didn't!?

● Do **not** use an apostrophe for the possessive adjective *its*, or for the possessive pronouns *yours*, *hers*, *ours* and *theirs*. Use:

    Has it eaten its dinner?

and *not*:

    *Has it eaten it's dinner?

Use:

    I think yours is the best.

and *not*:

    *I think your's is the best.

The confusion arises because the apostrophe is so often associated with possession:

    John's book.

In English *it's* always means *it is*.

There is a growing tendency to confuse *your* and *you're*. In the Leeds General Infirmary, for example, the following printed notice was displayed:

*Ladies, if there is any possibility of you're being pregnant, please tell the radiographer before treatment.

It should, of course, have read:

Ladies, if there is any possibility of your being pregnant, please tell the radiographer before treatment.

- Do **not** use question marks for indirect questions. Use:

He wondered where she had gone.

and *not*:

*He wondered where she had gone?

- Do **not** use a comma before a noun clause. Such a comma used to be the custom in English as it still is in German, but it is no longer acceptable. Use:

They knew that they should own up.

and *not*:

*They knew, that they should own up.

Use:

I realized what I should have done.

and *not*:

*I realized, what I should have done.

Use:

You asked what we intended to do.

and *not*:

*You asked, what we intended to do.

Use:

They admitted which one was faulty.

and *not*:

*They admitted, which one was faulty.

- Do **not** use commas to mark off defining relative clauses. Use:

Are you the one who is reading medicine?

and *not*:

*Are you the one, who is reading medicine?

Use:

I've read the book you recommended.

and *not*:

    *I've read the book, you recommended.

Use:

    Everything that she said was true.

and *not*:

    *Everything, that she said, was true.

Commas must be used, however, to mark off non-defining relative clauses. Use:

    Manchester United, of which you've heard, is expecting to win three cups this year.

and *not*:

    *Manchester United of which you've heard is expecting to win three cups this year.

Use:

    The houses, which we inspected, were in poor condition.

and *not*:

    *The houses which we inspected were in poor condition.

● Commas must **not** be used to separate discrete sentences. Use:

    She drove quietly into the car park; then she waited until the red BMW appeared.

or:

    She drove quietly into the car park. Then she waited until the red BMW appeared.

but *not*:

    *She drove quietly into the car park, then she waited until the red BMW appeared.

Sentences separated by commas are referred to as 'fused sentences'. They can appear even in articles associated with the English Language:

    It is estimated that one in five adults under the age of 25 has problems with literacy, often the problems are so severe as to amount to a severe handicap.

(We have refrained from attributing this quotation.)

Noam Chomsky has frequently claimed that the ideal grammar of a language would generate *all* the sentences of that language and *only* the sentences of that language. Our last word is a modified version of this. The ideal users of punctuation are those who use all the punctuation marks that are necessary for clarity and not one more.

Index